Robert Anderson Young

Sketchy Pages of Foreign Travel

Robert Anderson Young

Sketchy Pages of Foreign Travel

ISBN/EAN: 9783337292560

Printed in Europe, USA, Canada, Australia, Japan

Cover: Foto ©Andreas Hilbeck / pixelio.de

More available books at **www.hansebooks.com**

SKETCHY PAGES

OF

FOREIGN TRAVEL.

PUBLISHING H... ...TH.
BARB...

Entered, according to Act of Congress, in the year 1891,
BY R. A. YOUNG,
In the Office of the Librarian of Congress, at Washington.

Dedication.

To
The Beloved Wife and Children,
Who Have Been My Constant Companions in All the
Oriental and European Journeys,
This Book Is
AFFECTIONATELY DEDICATED.

A Note of Preparation.

EVEN in this day of superior facilities for the tourist, comparatively few of our people go abroad; and most of those who do travel appear to have no higher motive than self-gratification. True benefactors of the reading world are the select minority of travelers who study every thing from the best point of view, and faithfully chronicle the results in available form. To this honorable class, whose mission it is to please and instruct mankind, our author, Dr. Young, pre-eminently belongs. His tour of the far East, some years ago, was described with master-touch in his "Twenty Thousand Miles;" but this account of his recent eight months' excursion through Europe, when the experiences were altogether different and more stimulating, will give him a clearer title to the high rank we have assigned him. It is indeed a charming record of travel, and by him happily styled "Sketchy Pages." The auspicious sojourn in England and France, and the leisurely passage into Italy, Spain, Germany, Russia, Turkey, Denmark, Sweden, Norway, etc., afforded "sketchy" material without limit for this always cheery *compagnon de voyage*. With the genuine vim and elastic tread of youth, he leads us away from beaten paths, or makes old things seem new; for he sees with refined vision, catching and interpreting as by instinct the truest spirit of strange peoples and places. He is uniformly sage, terse, piquant in narration, while an air of purest altruism pervades his every sketch, and a rich deposit of historic lore underlies all.

Many have been anticipating this volume with pleasurable emotions. They enjoyed a foretaste of it in the letters given to the public from time to time during the progress of Dr. Young's journey. Read as a whole, these letters will be found to reflect with more distinctness the individuality of the writer. This characteristic quality amounts to real genius in Dr. Young, and its presence in these pages will impart higher relish to their perusal. Like Cowper's pilgrim,

> He travels, and expatiates: as the bee
> From flower to flower, so he from land to land.
> The manners, customs, policies of all
> Pay contribution to the store he gleans;
> He sucks intelligence from every clime,
> And spreads the honey of his deep research
> At his return—a rich repast for me.

That means for every one into whose hands this treasure of a book shall come. And now that the "note of preparation" has been sounded, let young and old, without number, enter upon this ideal "feast of good things." They will soon discover that no vain expectations have been raised by these commendatory words. JOHN L. KIRBY.

Nashville, September 3, 1891.

Contents.

	PAGE
"The Booking Office"	11
Ad Interim	16
The Voyagers	21
"My Journey into Spain"	28
Madrid	35
Seville	43
The Alhambra and the Mosque	51
Running Out of Spain	59
A Connecting Link	66
Second Connecting Link	74
Another Connecting Link	81
The Last Connecting Link	88
The German Capital	97
"Holy Moscow"	106
The Russian Capital	115
North of the Baltic Sea	124
Still Due North	131
Toward the Midnight Sun	139
London Day by Day	147
Paris Day by Day	157
Farewell to France	163
Resume	168

SKETCHY PAGES OF FOREIGN TRAVEL.

"THE BOOKING OFFICE."

EMERSON says that traveling is the paradise of fools. But Emerson says a thousand things that nobody pretends to understand or believe. In early life he made a pilgrimage to the genius of Carlyle, of Wordsworth, of Landor, and wrote his name several hundred miles up the Nile. Later, he lectured all over the British Isles and the United States. He ought to know how to pronounce on "globe-trotters."

New York, with the adjoining cities, is a wonderful hive of humanity. Put them all together, like we do Constantinople, and you have the largest city in the world but one. It takes Stamboul, Pera, and Galata on the European side, and Scutari on the Asiatic, to make up Lamartine's "predestined capital." So if you were to extend these corporation lines around New York, Brooklyn, Jersey City, and Hoboken, the place would be twice the size of Constantinople. The city on the Bosporus has no grander approaches than this on Manhattan Island. But New York lacks antiquity, history, and tradition. So we cross the seas.

I have spent the day examining steamers, especially those of the French line—"Transatlantique." Splendor is the word to use in a description of these ships. Surely naval architecture can do nothing beyond what I have seen to-day.

The French ought to be good sailors, especially those from Normandy. They come by their seamanship honestly—from the old Norse vikings, who plunged their prows into any port of Europe without saying, "By your leave." They do say, however, that when the storm is violent the Frenchman quits working and goes to praying. I heard this with pleasure, not knowing heretofore that devotion was one trait of his character. If I had heard that the louder the storm the more rapidly he "dances the cancan," I should not have been surprised. "O foolish Galatians, who hath bewitched you?"

I have been figuring with these Gauls today, and making some contracts. Necessity compels me to trade more closely than I did four years ago. Then every man fancies that he owns a reputation for keeping his word. Certain promises are out that the entire expenses of this trip shall not exceed $1,800, and that it shall embrace nearly every kingdom and capital in Europe.

For the best of reasons some of the happy party who traveled with us before will not be on this journey. But their places will be taken by other bright young people who want some information that reaches beyond pomp and millinery, and who are willing to give up surplus funds. Of the class who say, "Give me money, and I will deny you nothing," there will be no representative.

If Providence permit, we shall sail about the last week in January, so as to spend a winter month in the south of Spain, Andalusia. During the spring we shall be zigzaging about over historic and classical spots. The summer will be passed among the Russians, Finns, Swedes, Danes, Norse, and Lapps.

The best time to see the English—that quiet and inconsolable race—is in the early autumn.

Broadway is so exceedingly noisy and uninteresting to me that I came over to Jersey City to-night. This letter is the result. To-morrow I must look after the statue of Commodore Vanderbilt. I have a dozen bids from the sculptors here. There are two whose prices I can reach—thanks to the liberality of Nashville citizens. If I find them to be genuine artists, and not mere monument builders, I shall close a contract with one of them. (When I speak of Nashville liberality to any worthy enterprise, I wish to say that I have never seen it equaled anywhere else.) If a heroic bronze figure of the founder of our great university cannot be cast here, then it must be done in Munich, where the bronze workers of the world live. I hope also to see the grandson, Cornelius Vanderbilt, Jr., that I may gain some information that will benefit our re-investment committee.

I may hear Dr. Talmage on Sunday, though

I confess to conscientious scruples. He has been preaching for years to the largest congregation in the world, and yet they are not sufficiently Christianized and consecrated to rebuild a place of worship. They borrow the money, and give note and mortgage. "I reckon" he is a mere sensational performer. If I am strong enough to give Talmage the slip, then John Hall and Charles F. Deems. When a man puts a text at the top, I insist upon having the pure gospel.

I saw nothing new on the way to New York except Johnstown, and that looks rather old and dilapidated since the terrible disaster. *Good-night.*

New York, November 14, 1890.

AD INTERIM.

WHILE we were still at home, awaiting the departure of the French steamer, "La Bretagne," we enjoyed the company and profited by the instructions of some distinguished travelers. I mean *books*.

Of all the editors who travel, Henry M. Field is the most readable. There is a habit of authorship apparent in all he has done. It is manifest that he lives by his pen. 'Tis true he writes many pages about himself—the receptions, audiences, and entertainments offered him by orators, princes, and other grandees—yet he does it as delicately and modestly as one could expect. "Old Spain and New Spain" and "Gibraltar" will charm many a dreary and many a lazy hour.

Edward Everett Hale and his daughter have made themselves famous by a series of books called "Family Flights." I suppose the old Doctor furnishes the information and the daughter does the writing. Their "Family Flight o'er Spain" is equal to the one we read in Egypt, and that is praise enough. Histories of Spain are abundant, some of which we have read.

On the Scandinavian countries and peoples old Mr. Laing and Dr. Baird have furnished the "bottom facts." These venerable chroniclers have read their way back to Odin and beyond. What a realm of literature unknown to the men of average intelligence and culture! At the close of Dr. J. M. Buckley's big book—"The Midnight Sun, the Tsar, and the Nihilist"—I wrote on the blank page: "Bright, full, accurate, from beginning to end." W. R. Morfill's "Story of Russia" shows the hand of a laborious and delving scholar. He is the reader of the Russian and Slavonic languages in the University of Oxford. The young people of our party have all read "Fred Markham in Russia," "The American Girl Abroad," "Personally Conducted," and all the "Vassar Girls" series. I rather hesitate to say that I have spent one month on Buel's "Story of Man: A History of the Human Race."

2

My desire to visit the Iberian and Scandinavian Peninsulas is no fresh-born emotion. This is what I wrote in the spring of 1887: "To see all the countries of Northern Europe may bring me back in a few years from this time. If Providence permit, I must see the ancient seats of those great races who have run all over the world and who are at present enlightening and benefiting mankind."

In this meanwhile Bishop Key has been to see us. He is better than a book. There is always a room and a welcome and an admiration for him at our house. No day is so happy or so busy that the presence of Bishop Key does not improve it. Forty years ago we met in Griffin, Ga. We were rejoicing in our first white cravats and long frock-coats. The young man preached about Samson, and he has been getting stronger and stronger from that day to this. We entered our first General Conference together, and have met in the same body six times since. At the close of an election in 1882 I got the office, and Dr. Key dined with me. At the close of another election in 1886 Dr. Key was elevated to the episcopacy, and I dined with him. I heard his first sermon after ordination. We were in Norfolk, Va. The argument was the best I had heard for his theory of scriptural holiness. Very good. He can afford to advance high views of " holiness" so long as his life illustrates them with such " perfection."

Dr. R. K. Brown called the other day. He is our pastor at West End. Brown draws and edifies. They believe what he says. In the midst of the conversation he asked: "How does the sea appear to you when you are in the midst of it?" Henry M. Field has written a chapter on the "Melancholy Sea." To me it always looks cruel. So it did to Racine when it suggested that fine line:

Though cruel seas roll wide between us.

The Doctor then asked: "How does a ship appear when you are on it?" At the wharf it looks like a monster five hundred and fifty feet in length; in the midst of a wide waste of waters it seems like an egg-shell. And so we two talked of the dreadful fascination of the sea, and the wonders of naval architecture.

Eight of us have engaged rooms on the steamer "La Bretagne." Miss Dora Jones, of North Carolina, may stop in Paris. Dr. Bilbro would like to bring home a diploma from the Medical School of Vienna. The original six will remain together. "God be with you till we meet again."

January 30, 1891.

THE VOYAGERS.

THE best time to sail is when you get ready, quoth the veteran sea-captain; so we kept our appointment, and weighed anchor January 31.

Let us not fail to record, even at this distance of time and place, that elegant supper, that congenial company, and those solemn prayers from which we set out. Col. Thomas D. Fite knows exactly how to mingle the social and the religious element. He also knows how to kiss his way, right and left, out of a palace-car when the time comes for all friends to leave. There is no duplicate of the Colonel.

The sudden death of Secretary Windom was the sensation of the hour just as we pushed out from New York. He had come up from Washington to the city of great dinners to attend a banquet at Delmonico's, given by the Board of Trade and Transportation. He had responded to the first toast by making the speech of his life. He was dead in ten minutes thereafter—breathed his last while the applause of his countrymen died upon his ears.

What avails all our learning on this French greyhound of the sea? Officers and crew, waiters and passengers speak the French language so rapidly that we are bewildered. Wife was graduated from the "Old Academy," daughter has a B.A. degree from Dr. Price's, son was "trained" at Webb's, Miss Davis holds a diploma from Ward's, Miss Lester has studied French, Miss Hart was educated at Nazareth, Miss Jones at Greensboro, N. C., and Dr. Bilbro has two degrees —and yet, here am I, with three degrees, promising handsome "tips" to an English boy if he will stay around our table and interpret for us. But we shall improve, especially Miss Jones. She reads French with ease, and will soon learn to speak it. They report that Coleridge once thanked God publicly that he could not speak a word of such a language. We are not of his mind.

One rarely ever crosses the sea without meeting some new man. Capt. Schley this time. He and our Prof. Wharton were members of the same class at Annapolis. The Captain commands the ship "Baltimore," U. S. N. He gave us a thrilling account of his polar experience in search of Lieut. Greely and his crew. Capt. Schley is an "all-round-man"—talks with marvelous fluency on all subjects, from navigation to theology; and speaks English, French, Spanish, Italian, and what not. He is fond of music, games, and promenades. He does not dance. He believes, with Cicero, that no *man* in his senses will dance. The Captain and his wife have proposed to show us some attention at Gibraltar.

Another new man—Benjamin Constant, the great French painter. He was pleased with "Jack," the boy who swept the promenade deck—made a rough sketch of him on canvas. The picture sold immediately for six hundred francs. Fame is valuable in several respects.

Of course we had the usual concert on the

night before our arrival in Havre. The proceeds of all these entertainments are devoted to charitable purposes among seamen. On the Cunard line the money is given for the support of a sailor's hospital in Liverpool. On the French line it goes into the treasury of a life-saving society. On this occasion there was not a large company present, but their contributions amounted to 1,875 francs. The music was worth the money, for it was our singular privilege to hear a man singer who receives 2,000 francs a night in Paris. At the close an American lady made an effort to get up a dance, but she found the company too intellectual and cultured for that.

As our voyage was in the winter, we expected storms, and were not disappointed. We had two—one on Tuesday night and another on Wednesday night. The great ship rolled and pitched and quivered from end to end. But we knew Him who manages the deep, and thought:

> This awful God is ours,
>   Our Father and our love.

After an eight days' run we glided safely into the port of Havre, all well and eager to get another trip through sunny France.

The road from Havre to Paris runs through a part of ancient Normandy. The conductor gave us thirty minutes at Rouen, where we walked the platform, and talked of William the Conqueror, and especially how, in 1066, he went over to England, won the battle of Hastings, and established the Norman dynasty. Since then all "my lords" of England boast of pure Norman blood, and of an ancestry that came over with William's "fleet-load of thieves and pirates."

Here we are in Paris, reading the *Galignani Messenger*. From that veracious journal we learn that "King Carnival" is dead, and that only his ghost appeared on the streets and in the Grand Opera House on the night before Lent. *Ille mortuos est!* Thank the Lord!

This is Ash-Wednesday, the first day of Lent, and the British Parliament has resolved to sit two hours longer than usual. In France the places of amusement are closed for forty days; in England the Imperial Parliament moves straight along with accelerated motion in the transaction of business. The Frenchman lays stress on trifles; the Englishman is always practical. "The one invented a ruffle; the other added a shirt."

All the world has found out where we live. The Shah of Persia has resolved to make another tour. He will travel due east through India, across the Pacific, and from San Francisco to New York (taking in the World's Fair). Surely the people of the "Windy City" will not presume to entertain the King of Persia and *suite* at a yankee hotel! They must build and furnish a palace forthwith, and place it at his Majesty's disposal. Queen Victoria always gives him Buckingham when he visits her; and when he leaves, the royal abode has to be renovated from garret to cellar. "*The nausty Persians!*" "They don't daunce well."

A note to parents whose daughters are traveling with us: Your girls have learned the way to two places—*Au bon marche* and the *Magasins du Louvre*. Women are said to be fond of shopping. Look out for an expense account.

Our address for the next seven months will be Paris, France. Care of Thos. Cook & Son, *Place de l' Opera*.

Paris, February 12, 1891.

"MY JOURNEY INTO SPAIN."

TEN days in Paris, and we were off. Miss Ella Ford and her mother made our last hours in the fair city very happy. They invited sixteen Nashville people to "a tea." Among them were the queenly granddaughter of Chancellor Garland and the rosy-cheeked children of Mr. Ben Wilson. I would advise "Ben" not to call his daughters home, but to pick up their mother and come to Paris. The girls are anxious to see their parents, make a continental tour, and resume their studies. Miss Ford has ample quarters near the Arch of Triumph.

Our last day in Paris was Sunday. The forenoon was spent listening to the music in Notre Dame Cathedral. In the afternoon I went to hear Pere Hyacinthe—of course I did. Think of this great priest who once preached the lenten sermons in Notre Dame, with the royalty, nobility, and scholars of

France in front of him, now occupying a plain church in an obscure portion of the city! But he differed with Pius IX., and that settled the matter. When I was here in 1887, his congregation was not large. Now it fills the nave and four galleries. Every aisle is packed with chairs, and every foot of standing-room is taken. I saw scores of men with great, cliff-like brows, beyond which there must have worked busy brains. Why not congregate here? If the hearing ear comes close to the speaking tongue, it need not travel any farther than Pere Hyacinthe's. He is the prince of living orators.

I met a man the other day who ought to have some notice. It was at the mouth of a church. He helped my wife into a carriage and looked at me as if making the usual demand. I offered him half a franc, and he declined it pleasantly. The twin of this man does not live in all Europe. At the tomb of Napoleon a *valet de place* forced himself into our party and began to talk. More than once I ordered him to stop. The more I ordered, the faster he "lectured." At the gate he demanded three francs. I refused. He threatened to call the police. We drove off to the Eiffel Tower, and left the fellow fairly raging over a two-franc piece.

We left Paris on Monday evening, dusk, February 16. When our Spanish courier took charge of us at the Hotel du Louvre, I thought of St. Paul's words: "When I take my journey into Spain." We are going to the same Iberian Peninsula. A twenty-four hours' run brought us to Burgos, in the north of Spain, where I am writing this paragraph. We have had three meals on the way—the usual "coffee" at Bordeaux, luncheon at Irun, and dinner at Meiranda. We are spending a night and a day at this place, resting, "doing the town," and writing letters home. Of course we are across the Pyrenees. They are not so sublime as the Alps, or our own "Rockies," but the landscape is beautiful to the last degree. All the charms of nature are lavished on this romantic part of the Kingdom of Castile. The Cathedral at Burgos is the first of the four ecclesiastical wonders that we are promised on this circular tour of

Spain. We saw it at our leisure this morning, under the guidance of the sacristan.

Nobody is in a hurry down here. The Hidalgos wear their jaunty cloaks gracefully thrown over the left shoulder, and walk with stateliness; while beggars of every age, sex, and size swarm. The ladies protect their heads with the black mantilla, and the nursery maids wear snowy caps. They are all on the streets. At the eating stations the train stops from thirty minutes to an hour. The meal is served regularly in courses, with change of plates, knives, and forks. Wine flows, and smoke ascends from scores of cigars. It is now 8 o'clock, and I have rung *four times* for the morning fire. We get our coffee at nine. A French barber will shave you in five minutes; a Spaniard will fool and fondle around you for twenty-five.

We have seen the Escorial, pronounced by Castilians "the eighth wonder of the world." I have never known when to quote from Phillips's description of Napoleon before. The palace is "grand, gloomy, and peculiar." It is located at the foot of snow-crowned mountains, about thirty miles north of Madrid, with bad lands between it and the city. It is built of granite, in the shape of a gridiron. Everybody has heard the reason why. The walls are seventeen feet thick and five stories high. The structure is so large that it requires 14,000 doors and 11,000 windows. It employed an army of skilled workmen 22 years to finish it, at a cost of 6,000,000 Spanish crowns. The money spent on internal furniture and ornamentation could have been furnished by no man on earth 330 years ago, except Philip II., King of Spain. Viewed as a palace, a monastery, and a mausoleum, the Escorial stands alone in the history of architecture. We devoted the entire day to it, chaperoned by courier, castellan, and monk. A straggling village has grown up around it, whose population seems to be made up of soldiers, sisters, hotel-keepers, and beggars.

I should like to give the reader a more particular account of the Escorial if I had a "guide book," but there is not one in our traveling family. Every man who has read any thing knows that this palace was built when Spain was the richest kingdom in Europe. Ship-loads of silver and gold were constantly arriving from her colonial possessions in Mexico and South America. With untold wealth, an indomitable will, a gloomy disposition, and a vow to St. Lawrence for the victory of St. Quentin, we are not surprised that Philip created this wonderful palace. If the reader wishes to know any thing more, I refer him to "Souvenirs of Travel," two volumes, by Madame Octavia Walton Le Vert. By this means of acquiring information, he will have some delightful employment and *save* his money.

We are spending a week in the Spanish capital. Our young people are sending letters home and writing up their journals. They are all vigorous travelers and eager sight-seers. They lack neither appetite, health, nor humor.

Madrid is rich and gay. I have seen Central Park, in New York; Hyde Park, London; the Bois de Boulogne, Paris, each in "the height of the season;" but never have I seen, in one afternoon, so many splendid turn-outs as we saw in the *Prado* to-day. All the grandees of the capital seemed to be airing themselves. The descriptions we have read of their equipages are all true. We make an excursion to Toledo next week, and then return to the capital. I may write something more.

Please tell the assistant Agent that I have not seen an *Advocate* since January 26. I must hear from the Tennessee brethren. Of course they are living up to the New Testament standard, and the God of love and peace is abiding with them. But I want to hear from them. Send me the *Christian Advocate*. We have had no rain since we left the Atlantic. The climate is delightful.

Madrid, February 21, 1891.

MADRID.

WHAT of Madrid? The name is from a Moorish word, signifying a "current of air." It is certainly high and dry, and under the dominion of the winds.

As a town the origin of Madrid is prehistoric: as a place of royal abode it dates back only to Charles V.; as a capital to Philip II., who, in 1560, declared it the only court of the realm. While the kingdom of Spain has a population of 20,000,000, its capital city does not contain over 400,000 souls. It has no environs, except bad lands poorly cultivated.

On our arrival our courier quartered us at the Hotel de Russia. Here we have the best apartments ever offered us on this side. The food reminds me of the Palace Hotel in Santa Fe, New Mexico. That is kept by the descendants of these Madrilenos. Wife's olfactories are more troublesome than mine.

The servants are polite, obsequious, and slow. Fuel scarce. Lights dim.

Tourists usually go to the Royal Picture Gallery first, and devote one whole day to it—simply because it is the largest one on earth. Besides thousands of others, it contains the following numbers from the great masters, namely: Rubens, 62; Teniers, 53; Raphael, 10; Murillo, 46; Velasquez, 64; Van Dyck, 22; Titian, 42; Tintoretto, 34; Veronese, 25; Poussin, 19; and Claude, 10.

The next day we adopted our old plan, taking two open carriages and driving six hours. This afforded a general view of the churches, palaces, monuments, schools, libraries, industrial institutions, legislative halls, driving parks, and the rest of Madrid. The Madrilenos seem to be like the ancient Athenians: fond of sunshine and the latest news. From all I can see and hear, I judge that absolutism is forever dead in Spain. I can praise the American government as much as I please here.

Spain is a country where the Protestant religion has never been able to live. Pleasure, business, and labor are as manifest on the Lord's day as on any other day. On the way to three churches on Sunday, the English office of Thomas Cook & Son was the only place closed. The first place of worship I attended was one of the oldest in Madrid, ornamented with the rich carvings and furniture of the middle ages. Early mass was well attended by poor people. One old woman, having communed, came down the center aisle with a huge market-basket on her arm. About midway she interrupted a *devotee* for about one minute. The interview resulted in the loan of some market-money. In the second church a number of schools (male and female) came in. A fine, black-headed boy read some part of the service. The music was glorious. At the third church I heard a sermon. So now I have completed the list. In each Catholic country of Europe I have heard a priest, in his own language, deliver a sermon. They never preach from the great altar, but from a side pulpit. No Bible lies before them as with Protestants. They skip "thus saith the

Lord." They prefer "thus saith the Church." That is where all the ruin comes in to any body of Christians. For years I have felt perfectly impious whenever told of Church requirements, if they are not exactly in accordance with the letter or the broad and loving spirit of the New Testament. Do you quite understand me? But let me get back to these Romish priests. Their sermons are extemporaneous, and do not last over thirty minutes. They speak with great deliberation, and at the end of each paragraph pause longer than we do. They gesture too much.

The day on which I attended all these churches was bright and warm. The beggars were out in force. Women were sitting flat on the dark, dry sand. One young, emaciated creature had a baby in her arms. That brought my *pesetas* to the light. There I stood, and thought of the world-wide difference in condition between this Spanish baby and my darling grandchild out at the Kirkpatrick mansion in Nashville, and for little "Anna Hunter's" sake I gave the charity.

We have "permits" for the national palace, where the boy king, Alphonso XIII., and his Austrian mother live. We propose to use these passes to-morrow; but as the royal family are "in residence" we cannot hope to see much beyond the throne room, library, armory, state carriages, and the like. This palace is built upon the spot where the Moors first erected their Alcazar. It was the enterprise of Philip V., who resolved to rival that of Louis XIV., at Versailles. The material of the vast structure is white granite from Colmenar.

The visit has been made, and we saw more than we expected—even the queen and the little royalties. One of them, the boy, unites two of the oldest and highest houses of Europe—the Hapsburgs and the Bourbons. I hope this youngster may live and prosper. There was trouble enough about him before he was born. (See Henry M. Field.) This item will appear quite unimportant to all those who have not read the touching story of his young mother, who stood before the Spanish Cortes, and took the oath of regency for the unborn child.

Yesterday, bright and early, we went to Toledo. The farmers and gardeners were all out and busy with their spring work. Their land is not rich like the Netherlands. Toledo is a quaint, old, walled city. *Old*, did I say? If you should believe their chroniclers, the foundation of the town was laid about the time Adam and Eve made their appearance in the garden of Eden. The Alcazar is worth seeing. This vast stone palace was built by the Moors during the eight hundred years of their supremacy in Spain. It is well known that during that period they were the best educated and most highly cultured people in the world. The architecture of the Alcazar is one of the proofs. We saw two hundred workmen engaged in its restoration. Toledo is the seat of an archbishop. Its cathedral is the second of those four magnificent houses of worship of which all travelers write. The contents of the room containing the altar cloths and vestments, if sold at their nominal value, would build John Hall's church in New York. The swords made at Toledo are as celebrated as those of Damascus. All military men are loud in their praise of *toledos*. The hospitable captain of Greenland and the gallant colonel of High Street wear no swords; but, after our return, they shall have the pleasure of dispensing turkey from the point of a Toledo *carving-knife*. We returned to Madrid by the light of a full moon, and, as we approached the brilliantly illuminated city, thought of our future abode, and sung Philip Phillips's favorite song.

The mule is a popular animal here. They drive an omnibus with three abreast. They pull a heavy wagon with six in a row. Soldiers in gay uniform ride them. Even the queen's state carriage is drawn by four of these *dashing* hybrids. Wife wants a miniature donkey for our granddaughter's baby wagon, etc.

This country has had about six epochs— Iberian, Carthaginian, Roman, Gothic, Moorish, and Spanish. We shall take a stroll through the *Biblioteca* this afternoon, and glance at the curiosities, coins, books, and manuscripts of all these peoples. Then we leave for Seville, in the extreme South; hope the weather will be warmer in Andalusia. It is now 11 o'clock in the morning, February 25, and I am finishing this letter in the warmth of a good fire. We are well.

Madrid, February 25, 1891.

SEVILLE.

He who has not at Seville been,
Has not, I trow, a wonder seen.

FAIR Andalusia! We entered the extreme southern province of Spain last Thursday morning. We had been running the livelong night almost due south from Madrid, when we were aroused for a six-o'clock breakfast at Cordova. From there to Seville we noticed on all sides olive groves, orange orchards, cactus hedges, and palm-trees—all semi-tropical. This is the country where the Moors delighted to live, and which, for eight hundred years, they made flourish like a paradise. The country is level as a prairie, in a high state of cultivation, and dotted with charming white villages. It is watered by the Guadalquivir and its tributaries. We shall need no more fires, shawls, or cloaks while we are in this region.

A city founded by the Phenicians before

Romulus and Remus were born, encircled with walls built by Julius Cæsar, and where the Emperors Trajan and Theodosius were born, may well claim to be one of the oldest cities in Europe. Such is Seville; and yet it is in as perfect "repair" as Paris, and fully as clean. We are in the heart of the city, at the Hotel de Paris, on the Plaza del Pacifico.

The great square where the Cathedral now stands has always been occupied for religious purposes: first, a heathen temple; then, in the early days of Christianity, a church; in the year 1163 the Mohammedan Abu Yousef erected on the spot a noble mosque, which was pulled down two hundred years afterward. The present vast Gothic structure then arose. The Chapter of the Cathedral assembled in July, 1401, decided on erecting a church "so large and beautiful that coming ages may proclaim us mad to have undertaken it." They certainly succeeded. To give you an idea of its size, I may mention that *a small space* on the inside is given up for an orange orchard, covering an acre or two of ground. The present bell-tower, Giralda, is the minaret of the ancient mosque. We were all on the top of it this afternoon, feasting our eyes on the plains of Andalusia and the winding course of the Guadalquivir. There are some interesting things to be seen in the interior: original letters of Christopher Columbus, written with bold and graphic hand, the massive silver tomb of his son, Ferdinand, etc. We noticed a number of families amply and comfortably quartered in the various stories of the bell-tower. They are not disciples of Malthus either, but believe in the divine command—judging from the number of cradles and children visible. Talk of "high livers!" Here they are, "living higher" than those who dwell on the top of St. Peter's, at Rome. (See "Twenty Thousand Miles.")

Near by is the gorgeous Alcazar, covering many acres of ground. This is a palace built by the Moorish kings in the days of their refinement, wealth, and power, when their architects were as famous as their scholars. It is in as good condition to-day as it was when the Moors left it, for after their final expulsion, 1492, Ferdinand and Isabella restored and beautified the royal residence for their own occupancy. It was still further embellished by Charles V. on the occasion of his marriage to Isabel of Portugal. I am glad we have seen this perfect specimen of the Arabesque, with its gardens, and labyrinths, and kiosks, and pavilions, and grottoes, baths, lakes, Neptunes, tritons, under-ground fountains, and all else, before we wander next week amid the ruins of Alhambra. It is difficult to keep our young people away from the Alcazar. They never dreamed of such a human abode. I have not heard of Louvre, or Luxembourg, or Palais Royal, or Escorial, or even Queen Christina's marble home since they saw this royal establishment. They will be reading "Washington Irving," and such like, until they—get married. Let us hope that they may select men of culture and refinement, who will *lay out some money* on books, and encourage them to read on.

I brought them down from these elegant altitudes this morning, when I put them on a tram-way and carried them out to the *Fabrica de Tabacos.* There they saw 3,000 poor women and girls making cigars and cigarettes. While they worked with flying fingers they chattered like so many Spanish magpies. The building in which they assembled is a vast government structure, surrounded by a moat and exceedingly pleasant gardens. A man who can smoke a cigar after seeing one made is like myself: he can stand any thing. I think I said, not long ago, that Spaniards do not hurry. Here are these laboring-women, who can barely earn one *pesata* (20 cents) in a whole day, coming to their tasks at 11 o'clock. We arrived at 10 o'clock, to see them coming in from all quarters, leading children, carrying lunch-baskets, babies, and various *impedimenta.* One lively, little, black-headed Senora had a pair of twins—one in each arm. Away went wife's coppers!

After all this, we were in proper frame of mind to take two open carriages and drive through the Alameda and Las Delicias, to visit the University, the House of Pilate, and the palace of Duke de Montpensier. Thus we have passed the week in this bright old town.

Fair is proud Seville; let her country boast
Her strength, her wealth, her site of ancient days.

We did not cross the river to see Triana, where the gypsies live, or to explore the ruins of Italica, a city founded by Scipio Africanus.

Later. This is the Lord's day, and I am just in from Church. Forasmuch as I never could learn, in a Romish Church, where the apostolic ceremonies end and the pagan ceremonies begin, I thought it safest to abstract myself, and engage in mental devotion; praying to the Father, in the name of Christ, to direct me in all things by the light of the Holy Spirit. I am candid enough to admit that this is nearly all the religious direction I want from any source. The only theological book that ever suited me exactly is the New Testament. That I accept without hesitation. Such works as Calvin's "Institutes" have done the cause of true religion more harm than all the infidel literature from Porphyry and Celsus down to Ingersoll. Nobody believes in Calvin's God to-day. The old-timers are all dead. I knew the last one. His name was Andrew Vance. I once heard this dear old fatalist talking to a dying parishioner on the blessings of "election." What of the doom of "reprobates?" thought I. Dear Presbyterian friends, give us a revised Confession of Faith that magnifies the *love* of God, even if you have to put it in a "footnote."

I read with pleasure, from the *London Times*, that great interest has been aroused by the arrangements which have been made for the celebration of the Centenary of John Wesley's death, at City Road Chapel, on March 2, and the following days of the week. The Wesley Statue will be unveiled by the President of the Wesleyan Conference, the Rev. Dr. Moulton, at 11 o'clock on the morning of March 2. This ceremony will be followed by a public meeting in the City Road Chapel, to be addressed by Archdeacon Farrar and several representative Wesleyan ministers and laymen. At 3 o'clock the Rev. Dr. Moulton will deliver the Centenary Sermon. In the evening a public meeting will be held, to be addressed by the Presidents of the different Methodist Conferences in Great Britain and the Vice-president of the Irish Conference. On each succeeding day of the week, excepting Saturday, a sermon will be preached at 3 o'clock P.M. by a representative of one of the other Non-conformist bodies, and a public meeting will be held in the evening. Dr. Dale, of Birmingham, will be the Congregational preacher; Dr. Clifford will preach as a representative of the Baptists; and Principal Rainey as a representative of the Free Church of Scotland. This Centenary will also be marked by the publication of several volumes by the Wesleyan Book-room, bearing on the life and work of John Wesley and the growth of the Methodist movement.

Times have changed since March 2, 1791. "What hath God wrought!"

Seville, March 1, 1891.

THE ALHAMBRA AND THE MOSQUE.

THIS opening sentence is written in the Alhambra—in the room where Washington Irving registered in 1829. Hither came he in the *suite* of some titled gentleman in those days. The names of the aristocratic people have passed into oblivion; the man of genius is known the world over. "Ever thus."

In a few days after the arrival of Mr. Irving, the Governor of the old palace vacated his apartments, and tendered them to the quiet stranger. Here he indulged in those reveries and engaged in those researches that resulted in that charming book, "The Alhambra." Who has not read it? Venders of articles hereabouts will offer you an edition of it in any language you may chance to speak or read. I saw three translations. They offered us an American edition, supposing, of course, that we spoke a language differing from all others. There are three apartments in the Alhambra that were occupied by Mr. Irving: a library, a bed-room, and a dining-room. Here he not only wrote "The Alhambra," which has made the place known to the world, but I dare say, formed plans for the "Conquest of Granada," and "Mohammed and His Successors," and gathered the materials for those books. I can conceive of no better spot in Spain for the study of the romance, legends, traditions, and history of this wonderful country.

When we were at Stratford-upon-Avon, years ago, we stopped at the Red-horse Hotel. It had a room in it filled with *souvenirs* of Washington Irving. Here we are at a hotel bearing his name. It is so full of American tourists that my traveling family is scattered about in rooms on the second and third floors. Two old gentlemen from New York have big incomes at home and sprightly young brides with them. The brides read the guide books, and then tell their venerable husbands about places and events. "Who was Boabdil?" quoth one.

"The last prince of the Moorish Dominion in Spain," replied she, etc. The man from Baltimore knows exactly where he is and what he wants to see. The college professor has done Europe by the inch, and knows everything. The California gentleman wants the names of the good hotels in Seville and Madrid. "Many men of many minds," was our first copy. But the most amusing man is the uneducated and unread foreign traveler. "What is the difference between a mosque and a cathedral?" queried one to-day. "A mosque is a Mohammedan temple; a cathedral is used for the worship of Christ."

Granada is a large and interesting city—capital of the province of the same name—with a long and marvelous history. It is in the extreme South, with nothing between it and the Mediterranean Sea but the Sierra Nevadas. Their tops are covered with perpetual snow, and, forasmuch as most of the rooms in the Washington Irving Hotel are without fire-places, we are here entirely too early for comfort. When you ask about any manner or custom here, the invariable reply is, *cosas de España*. We have concluded that it is the custom of Granada to be without fuel.

This place was greatly favored by Ferdinand and Isabella, whose armies drove the last Moors out. Here they built the Royal Chapel, which is now their mausoleum. They rest side by side. In their day a new world was added to the dominions of Spain, to be lost nearly four hundred years thereafter by another Ferdinand. The sacristan shows you a golden casket, which contained the jewels pawned by Isabella to raise money for the expedition of Columbus. Some women know what to do with jewels.

The Alhambra has always been the royal abode of Granada. It is a palace, or rather a congeries of palaces, commenced by the Moorish kings, and finished, or disfigured, by Charles V. It covers many acres on a precipitous height overlooking the city. It it mostly in ruins. Some parts of it have been beautifully restored. The architecture is Saracenic, with infinite details and indescribable beauty. But the gardens, towers, fountains, pavilions, grottoes, over-ground and under-ground water-falls are more wonderful than the buildings. There is no other such ruin in the world. I am saving the whole subject for a lecture when I return.

Was there ever a people so leisure-loving and pleasure-loving as the inhabitants of Spain? Each man seems to be enjoying his *dolce far niente*, so that when he is old he holds out his hat for charity. Well, it is "*cosas de Espana.*" The most restless creature in the world is an American on a Spanish train. We started from Granada to Cordova early in the morning, and arrived late at night. The distance is about one hundred miles. Wonder if one man ever "credits" another in this country? He would have the pleasure of scheduling his outstanding accounts in his will. I requested a landlord to make out my bill each day and send it to the lunch-table. He hesitated, but finally agreed to do so if I would pay for the government stamp (ten *centimes*). He kept it up two days, and after that neglected it. He reminded me of the Nashville man, who was opposed to "settlements," even if the money was coming to him.

What shall I write of Cordova? It certainly contains a mosque which is the largest place of worship ever erected in honor of the only true God. It was built by Abdurrahman I., and was converted into a Christian church by Charles V. We have been wandering through it all morning, and feel too much wearied to write about it in detail. The founder resolved to erect a structure that should rival the Kaaba of Mecca in holiness, and the great mosques of Damascus and Bagdad in size. Our courier, Mr. Volonte, has seen the one in Damascus, and tells us that this surpasses it in every respect. The priests were conducting the morning service when we entered. The music that sighed, and wailed, and rolled through the vast inclosure seemed to come from the upper and heavenly choir—now loud, as from numbers without number, and then sweet, as from angelic voices uttering happiness and joy. O may we all finally meet in the great temple along whose aisles God's footsteps are ever heard!

As this letter is made up of hurrygraphs, you will allow me to close it with something better. On entering this place Mrs. Le Vert exclaimed: "And this moldering and crumbling city is Cordova! Cordova the learned and the wise; Cordova, so prosperous under the Carthaginians, and so famous under the Romans—the native city of the philosopher, Seneca, and the poet, Lucan; the city which gave to Rome her bravest soldiers, and which clung the longest to the fortunes of Pompey! After the Romans came the Gothic rule, and then the Moorish dominion, when Cordova was spread over these plains, and one million was the number of its inhabitants. While nearly all the rest of Europe was engaged in frightful wars, literature, the sciences, and the fine arts flourished in this favored city. Within the mosque is a forest of hundreds and hundreds of pillars and columns of marble, of jasper, of porphyry, brought, many of them, from the ruins of Carthage, from Asia Minor, and even from Rome. There is a perfect labyrinth of these pillars, while far above is the delicate tracery of the roof, almost like the foliage of trees." Cordova has been repaired since Madame Le Vert's day.

Cordova, March 6, 1891.

RUNNING OUT OF SPAIN.

ON our last morning in Cordova we strolled across the old Roman bridge to admire the massiveness of Cæsar's architecture, and thence through the immense mosque to hear the music float. Our young people are always ready for a ramble, for the tram-cars and carriages, or a sail on the waters. Meanwhile, each one journalizes every thing. It was from a journal like one of these that a very popular book of travels was produced about three years ago. Good luck to Lenamay!

On the long run from Cordova to Valencia, by the way of Alcazar and Albacette, we were compelled to infringe on the Lord's time until breakfast Sunday morning. We have never done so before; may we never be compelled to repeat it! The people were at work just as usual. Women were washing clothes, boys tending the flocks and herds, men planting and plowing, teamsters hauling, and mechanics building houses. All this grows out of the teachings of Roman Catholicism. Such a development of the religion of the "holy, harmless, and undefiled" Christ!

Spain is an undulating country; everywhere mountains, or hills, are in sight. Still there are vast areas of cultivable land. It looks somewhat poor and dry now. We have had one shower in thirty days. The olive is the great wealth of the southern portion, and there seem to be oranges enough to supply "the rest of mankind." All travelers write of the fine horses of Andalusia; we saw none.

We spent two days in Valencia at a very pleasant hotel. They say over here that "in America the traveler has to please the hotel; in Europe the hotel must please the traveler." There is some little ground for such a remark.

Valencia has been called the Sultana of Spanish cities. We saw nothing remarkably *queenly* about the place. It is a flourishing commercial town on the shores of the Mediterranean, with the usual narrow, winding streets and suburban drives. The Spanish gentleman must have three things—his cloak, his opera box, and his drive. Without these he is nobody. He may sleep in a back room, and live on broth, or at a soup-house; but if he can purchase these three luxuries he holds his social position—maintains his rank.

The history of the Province of Valencia is that of its capital—Carthaginians, Romans, Goths, and Moors have, in succession, possessed this fair land; and although it derived benefit from each, it is especially indebted to the Moor, who loved it, and lavished on it his gold and blood. Under the Moslem rule Valencia became the garden of Spain, and here the Moors placed their paradise. They called it "The Country of Mirth." The Cid, the great hero of the Spanish historical romance, wound up his career at Valencia. We saw his bones at Burgos. *May be* they were.

Thence due north to Tarragona. The railroad runs right along the shores of the Mediterranean Sea. In some places a tidal wave would overflow the track. Tarragona is admirably situated on a limestone rock, 800 feet high, and sloping to the sea. The climate is delicious, genial, and so wholesome at all times that the Roman Prætor used to make it his winter residence. But Roman remains here are considered *modern*. On the way to the Cathedral, in the picturesque Plaza, you may drink water from the ancient Phœnician well. Carthaginian "antiquities" are abundant. The Cathedral of Tarragona is a sort of Escorial, and contains the ashes, lately removed from Problet, of several mighty kings and queens of Aragon. Sculpture has not been despised or neglected in Spain, as monuments and statues frequently attest.

I fancy the reader ready to exclaim: "Will they never get away from the Romans?" Never, until we enter the dominions of the Tsar, or skim around through the Scandinavian Peninsula. The Romans encircled the Mediterranean Sea. Some day it will be difficult to get away from the English and Americans.

If you are in search of a "queenly" city,

come to Barcelona. It is the largest city in Spain, and by far the most beautiful. The Hotel of the Four Nations is unsurpassed in Europe. Barcelona was founded by Hamilcar 237 years before Christ, and is so favorably situated that it has never gone to decay. Ataulphus, the first king of the Goths, chose it as his court, and made it the capital of Hispana-Gothia. While Toledo is the Pompeii of Spain, this commercial emporium is solid as Glasgow.

When the Modern Language Association met in Nashville, one of its members referred to his two years' study in Barcelona. This remark attracted our attention to the university. It is a conspicuous pile of buildings of *quasi-*Byzantine character, dating from 1873. While leaving much to be desired in the way of curriculum, this is, perhaps, the most advanced of all Spanish universities. The institution contains a staff of really enlightened professors, 2,500 students, and a library of 200,000 volumes. There are over eighty primary schools attached to it. Would not Vanderbilt rejoice over eighty such training schools as the Webbs'? When we drove up in front of the university this morning, it was about 11 o'clock. There stood hundreds of plainly dressed young men waiting for the professors to appear. They have no use for early hours here, except to lie in bed.

We have at last seen a monument to Christopher Columbus worthy of his name. It stands on the wharf of Barcelona, the right hand of the figure pointing to America. We thought it surpassed Nelson's Pillar on Trafalgar Square.

On quitting Barcelona, in July, 1844, Washington Irving gave his opinion of the city thus: " I leave this beautiful city with regret. Indeed, one enjoys the very poetry of existence in these soft Southern climates which border on the Mediterranean. All here is picture and romance. Nothing has given me greater delight than occasional evening drives with some of my diplomatic colleagues to those county seats, or *torres*, as they are called, situated on the slopes of hills, two or three miles from the city, surrounded by groves of oranges, citrons, figs, pomegranates, etc., with terraced gardens gay with flowers and fountains. Here we would sit on the lofty terraces overlooking the rich and varied plain, the distant city gilded by the setting sun, and the blue sea beyond. Nothing can be purer and softer and sweeter than the evening air inhaled in these favored retreats." All our opinions agree with Mr. Irving. To-day, when I mentioned our early departure for Marseilles, I thought there would be a mutiny among the youngsters.

No country on earth, except Egypt and Syria, has ever interested and instructed me like Spain. But there will be no more letters. There may be none from Italy, Austria, Switzerland, or Germany. I visited those countries in 1886-87, and wrote my observations then. (Read "Twenty Thousand Miles.")

Letters are beginning to reach us, but no newspapers yet. Kind regards and best wishes.

Barcelona, March 12, 1891.

A CONNECTING LINK.

FORASMUCH as we are on our way from Spain to Russia, it may be well enough to supply a connecting link in the form of a diary.

March 12.—Our train is running along the shores of the Mediterranean. "Sunny France" indeed! We can see leagues of snow on the mountains to the left. The winter has been awfully severe in Europe, and it still lingers. We see the women at work in the fields. The army of Spain is large enough to preserve order at home. The standing army of France is the largest on earth. The able-bodied Frenchmen are there. It was dark when we reached Marseilles. We shall remain in this stately old city four or five days. We need rest and the services of a laundry maid. Did not the letters from home pour in upon us this evening! We are all happy. I am glad Dr.

Erwin's meeting resulted so gloriously. He and Blanton are invincible.

March 14.—A new French general has just arrived and taken command of the troops stationed at this place. He reviewed them this morning, while a steady rain came down on their gay uniforms. The column reached from our hotel out to the railroad station. A French soldier wears a bright-red cap with the number of his regiment glittering in front of it. He wears a deep-blue coat with red shoulder straps and cuffs. His baggy trowsers are red likewise; boots black; gloves white. Taken altogether he is a fiery-looking individual, but the German manages to whip him.

March 15.—All things come to those who wait. We have been waiting nearly two months for the privilege of entering a Protestant church. It was offered us to-day, and we all enjoyed it. "How sweet to the soul is communion with saints!" There are many Protestants in the south of France: at Montpelier, at Nimes, at Arles, at Avignon, and here at Marseilles, descendants of the old Huguenots. The service was conducted by Rev. Mr. Skeggs, of Oxford. Like all Englishmen, he gave ample time to it. We have attended English Churches in America, Europe, Asia, and Africa, and in all places they required a full hour and a half. Why not? They read long scriptures, and sing hymns " clear through." They go through the Commandments and all the creeds. The clergyman to-day not only prayed for the queen, the Prince of Wales, the royal family, Parliament, bishops and other clergy, army and navy, all sorts and conditions of men, health, wealth, and long life, and else; but he even included the President of the United States, and Mr. Carnot, who presides over the French Republic. I do not know whether the gentleman can *preach* or not. He *read* a capital exegesis, sixteen pages in length, wherein he clearly maintained the supreme divinity of our Lord. You can always trust an English Churchman on the text: "Before Abraham was I am." In America it is safest to wait until you hear him, especially in New England.

(After our quiet family prayers we shall sleep well.)

March 17.—We are on the "Riviera Route"—that picturesque and romantic country bordering on the sea, from Marseilles to Genoa. The great earthquake of 1887 shook this region terribly. The towns are all winter resorts for the grandees of the north of Europe, and they are indescribably beautiful. Architecture, art, and landscape gardening have done their best work along here. Napoleon I. connected his name with Toulon. Queen Victoria spends a part of her winters at Cannes. Mr. Spurgeon comes to Mentone. The German royalties are partial to San Remo. All the gamblers flock to Monte Carlo. Tourists generally stop at Nice (pronounced *Nees*). An elderly man must not walk on stilts. I must not attempt a description of the palaces, chateaus, cottages, promenades, and sylvan solitudes of this place. A rain-storm is raging just now. The clouds are inky black. The tempestuous heavens pour down torrents. The thunders roll along the shores and far over the billowy sea. But we are comfortably housed, and Nice will be bright again to-morrow.

March 20.—We have completed the Reviera, and are literally "basking in the sunshine" of Pisa. Even in Italy there never was a more beautiful day. While the young people were climbing the Leaning Tower, and doing other duties of travel, I sat on the steps of the cathedral. A carriage drove up, such as I had never seen outside of royal stables. When the service closed, I expected the king and queen of this realm to enter it, when lo! a red-capped cardinal appeared. He and the attendant bishops filled the gorgeous conveyance. If the President of the United States were to attend church with such an array of horses, harness, drivers, and liveried footmen, no political party or combination on earth could re-elect him. Martin Van Buren tried certain showy ways while he occupied the White House. The halls of Congress rang with glowing descriptions of them. The newspapers teemed with ridicule. He was defeated.

March 22.—There are five cities in the

world that are called "holy:" Benares, for the Hindoos; Mecca, for the Mohammedans; Jerusalem, for the Jews; Moscow, for the Greek Church in Russia; and Rome, for all good Catholics. To each of these places devotees make pilgrimages at certain seasons. We are in Rome not as pilgrims, but according to a schedule of travel made out in America. This is "Holy Week." All nations, tongues, kindreds, and people are represented here. An archbishop from Madras appeared the other day. The most gracefully robed functionary I have seen is a Chinaman. The little fellow from Tonquin comes next. The city is full. Resources of public comfort are exhausted. Every hotel and *pension* is packed. The place where we are stopping is so crowded that the Americans have been offered a private dining-room without the usual "supplementary price." So the Hotel D'Allemagne has forced us to be "elegant." We have been writing and telegraphing for one week before our rooms were secured.

"Hail, holy Rome!" exclaimed a German pilgrim about the year 1510. His name was

Martin Luther. Before he quitted the place those thoughts entered his mind which resulted in the Protestant Reformation. To-day is Sunday. I went in search of a Protestant Church. There are many here. After getting lost several times, I called a cabman and succeeded. The house was large and comfortable, and was filled with devout worshipers. The service was altogether edifying. On the way home I noticed that offices and places of business were open as usual. The military bands were in full blast, cavalry prancing and soldiers marching. Carriage wheels glittered on every street, and the lovers of pleasure were all afloat. "Hail, holy Rome!" Your saints have managed to skip all the Commandments to-day: Palm-Sunday. In the evening we heard vespers in St. Peter's. No instrumental music. Only singing. Italy is the land of song.

Next Sunday is Easter day. Five days in advance, I offer this prediction: After all the solemn and pompous ceremonies in honor of the resurrection of our Lord are over, and the pope has blessed the people in front of St. Peter's, every theater, dance-house, and place of sin will be open and filled to overflowing. I acknowledge the good works of benevolence which the Romanists have done, but my observation teaches me that they have never learned to keep holy the Lord's day, or practice many Christian virtues.

March 23.—We have spent the entire day in "Old Rome." At the Colosseum, Arch of Constantine, and along the Via Sacra; at the Arch of Titus and through the Forum; at the Arch of Septimus Severus, and among the statues of the Capitol and the Pantheon, I have been talking to my traveling family on Roman history and antiquities. In this way we expect to occupy every day of the present week.

Rome, March 23, 1891.

SECOND CONNECTING LINK.

O Rome! my country! city of the soul!
The orphans of the heart must turn to thee,
Lone mother of the dead empires!

MARCH 24.—I have finished reading "The Romans a Hundred Years Ago." This must have been a dirty, dilapidated city, and filled with a desperate population. It is not so now. Within the present century, it has grown from 160,000 souls to half a million. I can name no city in Europe where so many magnificent structures are in process of erection. They are even embanking the Tiber like the Londoners have done the Thames and the Parisians the Seine. "The Eternal City," which has lived since 750 before Christ, has "taken a new lease on life." Look from the top of the capitol or from the dome of St. Peter's at the beautifully undulating country! It suggests health. Wine-drinkers all declare the water is not good. People who come here for dissipation complain of Roman fever. But whence the healthy men and women who have lived here for twenty-five hundred years?

After cabling our congratulations to the niece, Lenamay Green, we devoted the day to the palace of the Pope of Rome. St. Peter's "successor" lives in a much larger house than those usually intended for the shelter of Christian ministers. The building was commenced over one thousand years ago, and there has been time for enlargement since that date. The walls are 15 feet in thickness, and inclose 14 ample courts, 300 stairways, and 11,454 rooms. Leo XIII. is 82 years of age, and, like all great men, he is doomed to incessant thought and labor. In this respect he is the peer of Napoleon I. or Frederick the Great. The pope rises at six in the morning, and works far into the night. His only recreation is a drive through gardens of bewildering beauty, three miles in circumference. The old gentleman was never married; but his family, counting from the College of Cardinals down to the Swiss Guards, numbers 1,160 persons. Our business in the Vatican was to see more than a mile of frescoes, pictures, statuary, mosaics, and books. It will require another day to complete the job. If any critic should read this diary, and differ with me about the ancient foundation of the Vatican, let him remember that it existed in the time of Charlemagne, who inhabited it when he was crowned by Leo III. on Christmas-day, A.D. 800.

March 25.—We beheld service and ceremonies in the Pantheon. This magnificent temple of all the gods of "Old Rome" is now a Christian Church. It was erected by Agrippa 27 years before the Christian era. The Parthenon at Athens is shattered and in ruins, but the Pantheon is preserved. A.D. 608, Phocas, Emperor of Constantinople, gave it to Boniface IV., who consecrated it to the Virgin and Martyrs; hence its present name. The portico is supported by 16 columns of Oriental granite of a single block, with beautiful capitals. They support an entablature and a pediment of stupendous design. In the interior we find grandeur and elegance united. Being of a circular form, it is commonly called *La Rotonda*. Its diameter is 132 feet, and it measures the same in height. Its roof is all dome—the largest in the world. Like all pagan temples, it has no windows; the light comes from an aperture in the dome. In this temple are buried several celebrated artists, among them Raphael, the most famous of them all. Victor Emanuel, the " Unifier of Italy," was interred here in 1878. (This paragraph looks to me somewhat like a page in a guide book. Well, there shall be no more to-day.)

March 26.—Holy Week is passing away. Churches all open day and night. Service, ceremonies, music, marching, masses everywhere. Dignitaries of Church and State are thick as knaves. The Queen of Italy and the Duchess of Genoa assisted at the service to-day in the Church of the Sudario. In the afternoon her Majesty visited several churches where the sepulcher was exhibited. She made the pious pilgrimage on foot. I have heard of but one sermon. On Tuesday last, at the Vatican, Father Francesco da Loreto, of the Capuchin Order, preached the last of his Lenten sermons in the presence of the pope and the pontifical court. If the monk held forth the word of life, it was delivered in the right place.

The music has not met the expectations of the multitude of foreigners who are here, one piece excepted—*The Miserere*. We heard it twice—once in St. Peter's and again in St. John Lateran. There were 20,000 persons present at St. Peter's, and about 5,000 at St. John's. The choirs of these rival churches are led by masters of great celebrity. I know nothing of the science of music; but any man of sense or sensibility ought to be spiritually improved by listening to *The Miserere*. All descriptions of the execution and effect of this wonderful chant seem tame, except J. T. Headley's, in his "Letters from Italy." The reader is referred.

Easter Sunday.—We have used our time this morning to the best advantage. First to the Church of *S. Pietro Vincoli*. This church contains the world's masterpiece of statuary—Michael Angelo's "Moses." The service was dull, and we left. Next to the

Basilica, where the Bambino is worshiped, and on whose steps Edward Gibbon planned the "Decline and the Fall of the Roman Empire." Then to the Jesuit's Church for the sake of the music, of which there was none. After all this we had ample time to worship the Lord with the English Protestants. The clergyman maintained, in the usual way, the resurrection of Christ and of the whole human race. While speaking of the foundation of the Church he regretted that strong men like John Robinson and John Knox and John Wesley had been able to mar its unity. He told the burly English people that they were more capable of keeping Lent than any other nation—they were naturally a quiet, sober, sedate race. Thought I: "They may have capacity for fasting, but scores of them in Hotel D'Allemagne have the largest 'capacity' for breaking a fast I have ever seen." The house was full this morning—the last chair taken. The carriages of the aristocracy drove up late. Their liveried footmen came in with their masters and heard the sermon.

After to-night Holy Week is over. Plays

and operas are announced, and the races begin to-morrow. "Hail, holy Rome!" The gay turn-outs are already glittering on their way to the Pincian Hill drives. I wish I could be at a Methodist protracted meeting. I want to see somebody *in earnest*—talking about religion as if he believed in its truths.

March 30.—This is a good day for letters. The *portier* handed us a large package from America. I make my best bow to Col. Fite for four pages. His letter is like himself: agreeable, versatile, newsy. W. T. Turley, Esq., is in with two more. He ought to have a premium for letter-writing. He is next to Irving on a literary salmagundi.

We leave Rome to-day for an excursion to the island of Capri. It lies out in the Bay of Naples, just opposite the city, and in full view of Mt. Vesuvius. There we shall rest a little while on its shining shores, and then return to Rome. We have forty-six days yet at our disposal before the season for entering Russia or Scandinavia. Health still gushes from a thousand springs. Love to all.

Rome, March 30, 1891.

ANOTHER CONNECTING LINK.

APRIL 6.—We leave Naples—"*la Bella.*" The island of Capri is twenty-five miles distant from the Sea-wall. I mention a few of the excursions that may be made from its shores, giving the Italian spelling: Grotte-Bleue, Sorento, Castellammare, Pompeii, Herculanum, Mont Vesuve, and all the environs of Napoli. We took these delightful and instructive trips without hurry or weariness. The bay of Naples is usually quiet as a lake, and the little steamers are crowded with intelligent tourists from all lands. Bands of music everywhere, but no dancing.

We are again in the "Niobe of the Nations." Many of her children are dead, but Rome now lives and flourishes. The city is still called "*L'Eterna.*" My *last* view of this world center was taken from the Church of San Maria Maggiore, whose foundations were laid away back in the first ages of Christianity.

April 7.—Reached Florence, the city of fair flowers, and certainly the flower of fair cities. All that nature can furnish or art create may be found here. We abide for several days.

The ninth General Conference of the Christians of all nations, known as the Evangelical Alliance, is in session here. Think of free discussions on religious matters in the heart of Italy! There are two Churches represented here *now*. On one side is the dominating papacy, which, by reason of its own special dogma, does not allow controversy. It must be accepted or not *just as it is*. The people, or at least a majority of them, accept it in form; but if statistics could be drawn up of the *consciences*, how many among those who are registered as Roman Catholics in name would appear as real Catholics? How many are there, in fact, who openly admit that their religion is nothing else than a religion of habit?

On the other side, moved by a noble spirit of charity, several Protestant denominations, from various parts of the world, have sent members to Italy to awaken the religious spirit. These learned men, hard-working, patient, and benevolent, have done a great deal of good. They have founded churches, gathered around them groups of sincere believers; but a real religious *movement* has not been stirred by them yet.

Steps toward reform in Italy were taken about the end of the 15th century by Savonarola and others, and again in the beginning of the 16th century; but they were checked at once, and not by Italians only. Now, near the close of the 19th century, a new reform ought to be started by Italians in Italy.

A part, small but compact, of the Italian population, since time immemorial, constitutes a Church which could gather around it all those dissenting from the Vatican doctrines, but who intend remaining Christians. That glorious population, which has for centuries inhabited those valleys running down from the Cottian Alps, between the sources of the Po and the Dora; which has upheld inviolate its belief through persecutions of every kind; which has been rendered famous by historians and sung by poets from Milton to Mamiani—could it not be the center of Italian reform? The Waldenses are meant.

Several delegates from America were especially cordial to me, among whom was Bishop Walden. Some went so far as to offer me a permanent seat, but a ticket of admission was all I desired. Suppose you print it in words and figures as follows:

Alleanza Evangelica.

IXa Conferenza internazionale.

Dal 6 agli 11 Aprile 1891.

(R. Peatro Tommaso Salvina, Via de'Neri.)

Biglietto d' Ingresso

Posti Resevati in 3a Fila.

Il Presidente del Comitato Fiorentino.

P. Geyonat.

The theater in which the Alliance met was filled from floor to ceiling, including four galleries. After the President announced the hymns in several different languages everybody sung. Then came the opening prayer in a foreign tongue. Indeed, I heard but one speech in English, and that was delivered through an interpreter. The speaker was an American and a Methodist. His subject, the "Doctrine of the Holy Spirit."

While I am writing, the *Roman Herald* has been brought in. Under the head of "General News" it says: "The ninth International Conference of the Evangelical Alliance was inaugurated last week in Florence. A great number of ministers and evangelical notabilities, representing *twenty different nationalities*, were present. After the opening formalities had been gone through with, it was proposed to send a telegram of respectful homage to King Humbert. The proposal was voted immediately, amidst enthusiastic applause.

"In reply the following letter was sent to the President of the Congress:

"His Majesty the king received, with great pleasure, the respectful homage accorded by the representatives of the religious faith professed by a Subalpine people (Waldenses) endeared to him for their faithful loyalty to the House of Savoy. Our August Sovereign thanks in special manner all the strangers assembled, for their good wishes, and invocations to God for Italy's prosperity; and is happy to know that when they return to their homes they will take with them feelings of sympathy for this country and retain a pleasing remembrance of it. His Majesty the King wishes to express his cordial feelings toward the Congress. The General Secretary,

"RATTAZZI."

Another learned body has just gone from Florence. The gentlemen were scientists from London. They all stopped at the Anglo-American Hotel, where we are also lodging.

There are six American Episcopal Churches on the Continent of Europe, established at the following places: Rome, Paris, Nice, Dresden, Geneva, and Florence. They are building another at Lucerne.

April 12.—Attended the American Church expecting to hear Dr. Tiffany, of New York, or Dr. Philip Schaff, but heard a vastly inferior man. The paragraph on Stonewall Jackson must have been written for the especial benefit of Southern ears. Wife is determined not to hear him any more. The men of our latitude have accepted the results of the Civil War, and are behaving admirably; but the women who were once refugees, and tasted sorghum and corn-bread, are resolved "to die game;" or at least they will tolerate no eulogy on Stonewall Jackson that contains the word "misguided."

April 13.—We are shipped for Venice, the "City Built on the Sea." We can afford to remain there for some time. The "tarif" at the Victoria Hotel is very moderate.

The *Christian Advocate* is beginning to reach us with some regularity. News from a far country; how delightful it is! Especially if that country is our home. I hope John Howard Payne is in heaven. I feel like I would be willing to turn an angel out to let him in.

En Route, April 13. 1891.

THE LAST CONNECTING LINK.

APRIL 20.—For a week we have been floating along water streets and alleys, gazing at the beauties and triumphs of architecture, walking over bridges, listening to music, and occasionally hearing an eccentric Scotch Presbyterian preacher.

My friend Hill is exceedingly fond of Ruskin. For his gratification I quote a paragraph from the "Stones of Venice:" "The State of Venice existed thirteen hundred and seventy-six years from the first establishment of a Consular Government on the island of the Rialto to the moment when the general in chief of the French army of Italy pronounced the Venetian Republic a thing of the past. Of this period two hundred and seventy-six years were passed in a nominal subjection to the cities of old Venetia, especially to Padua, and in an agitated form of democracy, of which the executive appears to have been intrusted to tribunes, chosen one by the inhabitants of each of the principal islands. For six hundred years, during which the power of Venice was continually on the increase, her government was an elective monarchy, her king or doge possessing, in early times at least, as much independent authority as any other European sovereign, but an authority gradually subjected to limitation, and shortened almost daily of its prerogatives, while it increased in a spectral and incapable magnificence. The final government of the nobles, under the image of a king, lasted for five hundred years, during which Venice reaped the fruits of her former energies, consumed them, and expired."

The work accomplished in the early days of Venice must have been stupendous. Her canals (streets) were made and preserved. Man's enterprise had to do battle with the assailing ocean. Forests of piles had to be sunk to hold the shifting land together. In the lapse of time the huts of Veneti gave way to marble palaces, and the group of desolate islands, stolen from the sea, was converted into one of the chief cities in the world.

The fifteenth century witnessed the culmination of the greatness of Venice. From its earliest days until the close of that century, step by step it rose higher and higher until the whole world acknowledged it as the center of commercial prosperity.

More. Here Galileo, in 1609, on a visit, while professor in the old University of Padua, invented the telescope; and having with it studied the stars from the summit of the Campanile of St. Mark, presented it to the doge. Here, too, at a subsequent period, Sirturi constructed an instrument of the same description, and used it on the same bell-tower. Here Ignatius Loyola, in 1536, organized, with his friends, the order of the Jesuits, and hence repairing to Rome, sought and gained the sanction of Paul III. to his enterprise. In Venice were born, or lived, or died, Titian and Tintoretto, Vittoria and Canova, Tasso and Marco Polo; and the dwellings they inhabited are yet pointed out.

At the opening of the seventeenth century

the first newspaper in the world appeared at Venice, and being sold for a coin called a *gazetta*, it thence took its name. Strange that the great "palladium of liberty" should have originated under the most jealous despotism that ever existed! At Venice, too, appeared the first bill of exchange and the first bank of deposit and discount.

Just see where this fondness for history is about to carry me! Don't I know "full well" that the more I write in this strain the less interesting will this diary appear in the estimation of the majority of the people? Wonder if my old friend Gov. Foote ever finished and published his "History of the Venetian Republic?" The pages I heard read were brilliant to the last degree. They reminded me of "John Lord's Lectures."

We left the unique city early this morning, and came to Milan by the way of Padua and Verona. The university buildings at the former place are "a sight" with age, and the tomb of Shakespeare's Juliet, at the latter, has been converted into a washing-tub. So we tarried at neither place.

Milan is the solidest city in Italy, and one of the largest. Three hundred thousand people are making money, and therewith seem content. Not a beggar appears! Of course we shall take the regulation drives and make the usual visits—to the "Miracle in Marble;" to the spot where the iron crown of Lombardy was placed upon the heads of Charlemagne, Charles V., and Napoleon I.; to the church containing the original "Great Supper," by Leonardo da Vinci; and to the Campo Santo and Crematory. Then we shall gather up our clothes, strap our valises, settle our bills, "tip" the servants of the Belle-Vue, and take leave of the fine arts of Italy forever.

April 23.—We are at Lucerne—the *shining* place. To get here we came through the wildest of all wild regions. When the St. Gothard railway begins to ascend the Alps, it climbs elevation upon elevation and height upon height so easily you think it may equal Hannibal or Napoleon, and cross over; but after awhile the train glides into a tunnel which runs under the highest peaks for about ten miles, and lets you out on the other side.

On the route from Milan to this place we left Lake Como and Lake Lugano on the right hand, Lake Maggiore on the left, and skimmed around Lake Lucerne. This is an old city. The inhabitants are the descendants of the prehistoric "Lake Dwellers." It has been raining all day. No difference. Let it rain on. The letters came from home, and along with them a beautiful picture of the charming and chubby grandchild. Wife is willing to have rain to-morrow.

Here we find the Lion of Lucerne, a celebrated monument executed by Lucas Ahorn, of Constance, after a model by Thorwaldsen, and completed in 1821. It is intended to commemorate the soldiers and officers of the Swiss Guard, to the number of eight hundred, who laid down their lives at the Tuileries in Paris, in defense of Louis XVI., in 1792. The men who died so bravely are perhaps destined to find a more lasting monument in the eloquent and spirit-stirring words of Carlyle: "Honor to you, brave men; honorable pity, through long times! Not martyrs were ye, and yet almost more. He was no king of yours, this Louis; and he forsook you like a king of shreds and patches. Ye were but sold to him for some poor sixpence a day, yet would ye work for your wages, keep your plighted words. The work was now to die, and ye did it. Honor to you, O kinsmen! Not bastards; true born were these men; sons of the men of Sempach, of Murten, who knelt, but not to thee, O Burgundy! Let the traveler, as he passes through Lucerne, turn aside to look a little at their monumental lion; not for Thorwaldsen's sake alone. Hewn out of the living rock, the figure rests there by the still lake waters, in lullaby of distant tinkling *Rance-des-vaches*, the granite mountains dumbly keeping watch all round; and though inanimate, speak."

April 25.—This is Saturday. We came to Schafhausen and stopped, simply because we never travel on Sunday. The Creator's plan is better than ours.

On the Lord's day we attended a Protestant Church of immense size. It was comfortably seated and well filled. The people were not coming in, strolling around, and going out all the time, as in the pewless cathedrals of Italy. John Hall's congregation in New York is not more prompt and orderly and devout than these Swiss Calvinists.

April 28.—After running out of Switzerland and crossing Lake Constance, we are spending several days in Munich, the capital of the kingdom of Bavaria. Among the cities of Germany, this holds the first rank as a city of art, possessing a greater number of monumental buildings, replete with valuable collections. "I will make of Munich such a city that whosoever has not seen it does not know Germany," once declared King Ludwig I., and he made good the declaration. It is certainly the most beautiful place we ever saw. (If I wrote a sentence like this in Barcelona, Spain, I now beg leave to take it back.)

April 30.—Spent the forenoon in the Royal Bronze Foundry, established in 1825 by King Maximilian I. The moment one enters he sees that America has availed herself largely of the work done here. The models of Washington, Jefferson, Webster, Clay, Benton,

Marshall, Everett, and dozens more are here, in the midst of emperors, kings, princes, authors, and generals. The chief of the establishment is a nobleman, in whose office I passed an hour. His calculations and propositions are more favorable than those made in New York. I shall return to his office to-morrow.

May 2.—This is the last paragraph I shall write in the form of a diary; for after stopping some days in Dresden, we go straight to Berlin. There, according to contract, a Russian courier will meet us. With him we shall travel through the Tsar's dominions and all Scandinavia. When I was a country boy, one of my few "manly accomplishments" was swimming. Early in the season I always dreaded to make the first dive. So now we hesitate about making our first plunge into a country so naturally cold and strange as the immense Empire of Russia. But the Lord is provident. So we have found him. Therefore we trust him with *implicit faith*.

Dresden, May 2, 1891.

THE GERMAN CAPITAL.

ON our arrival in Berlin I had, in small change, only about thirty marks. So, as soon as we settled down, I must see some bankers. It was about 1 o'clock. The International Bank was closed for lunch—*two hours*. I walked on to the Dresden Bank. Closed for lunch! They showed me the reading-room, where I found the *New York Herald* and other American papers. At 3 o'clock all the financial gentlemen appeared.

"Who speaks English?" quoth the customer.

"I do," said an officer.

"Can you give me German gold for English bank-notes?"

"We can."

Whereupon he wrote out a receipt on a piece of paper about the size of a leaf from a family Bible. It stated that the bank had received from me two five-pound notes,

Bank of England, for which I had been paid two hundred and two marks. The officer then went to the vault where the precious metal is kept, and remained about five minutes before delivering the gold. Two days afterward I went back for more money. All the banks were closed. It was Ascension Day. Suppose the banks of Nashville were to shut up every time the Roman Catholics or the Protestant Episcopalians choose to observe a "day!" What a number of holidays the officers and employees would enjoy! I write this paragraph for the consideration of Plater, Keith, Harris, Porterfield, Sperry, and the rest. They are just a little too energetic for any *German* use. Why rush yourselves to death, old gentlemen?

We have been to the Royal Art Exhibition. The artists of Berlin are celebrating the fiftieth year of their Association. Empress Frederick, mother of the Kaiser, is the chief patroness. Her late visit to Paris is known to all. The Exhibition grounds and buildings are "wonderful," as Bishop Keener would say. All lands where sculptors and painters flourish have "departments" here. Even distant "Amerika" has filled *two* rooms. And let it be said to our credit that no obscene figure appears upon any Western canvas. We are the decent people of the world. 'Tis true, we rise up early and lie down late, and hurry through life; we drive and strive and struggle to get rich, and refuse to enjoy ourselves unless we are "in easy circumstances;" but, compared with other nations, we are decidedly religious and decent.

The American flag floats *westward* from one pinnacle of the Exhibition building. One sight of the "stars and stripes" brought to memory a long-forgotten poem of N. P. Willis:

> Bright flag, at yonder tapering mast,
>   Fling out your field of azure blue!
> Let star and stripe be westward cast,
>   And point as freedom's eagle flew!
> Strain home, O lithe and quivering spars!
> Point home, my country's flag of stars.

When we were here four years ago, Prince William was living quietly at Potsdam.

Then he was two removes from the throne. Now he is an emperor, and, though quite a young man, seems to have mastered the whole trade of kingdom and lordship. (The history of heroes is the history of young men.) At that time Prince Bismarck was at the head of the government—an actual Dictator. Now he begs votes to elect him a member of the Reichstag, where he will appear as the opponent of the government. The most pathetic spectacle of antiquity is the great Belisarius begging an *obolus* at the gates of Rome. But Belisarius never posed as the enemy of his emperor. If Prince Bismarck had remained in retirement—*otium cum dignitate*—he would have gone down to posterity as the most powerful statesman of the nineteenth century. Now he loses henceforth.

What uncounted sums of money kingdoms and royal families expend in the building of palaces! I give the list of those I have seen here: The National Palace, Berlin; the Kaiser's private palace; palace of the Crown Prince; Castle of Charlottenberg; the National Palace at Potsdam; Sans Souci; New Palace; Marble Palace; and Babelsburg, besides others at watering-places, summer resorts, and on the Rhine. All these are at the service of the royal family of the kingdom of Prussia—a family that has never been accused of much splendor or extravagance, as Louis XIV. was. Add to this that the German Empire is made up of a number of kingdoms, dukedoms, princedoms, and free cities, and that each of these kings, dukes, and princes has more than one palace. The apartments of these palaces seem to be endless, and there are many single rooms that cost more money than the finest dwelling-house in Tennessee. Then look at the grounds, furniture, servants, guards, and you are ready to exclaim: "No wonder the common people are so poor and women work in the fields! Who blames such strong-headed men as Stahlman and John Ruhm for getting up and going out of such a country?"

While I am writing, intelligence reaches us from the courier who is to travel with us through Russia. His name is Clausen, a Swiss by birth, but thoroughly conversant with the Tsar's people. I hope our experience with him will lead us to speak, as all European people do, of "the fidelity of the Swiss." When, in revolutionary times, a "Guard" was placed in front of the palace of Louis XVI., Swiss were chosen, and they died for him. As one enters the Vatican in Rome, he passes between files of soldiers. They are the famous "Swiss Guards." The Republic of Switzerland could only be conquered by the death of the last Switzer. May our Swiss conductor prove to be a duplicate of William Tell, if we get into any danger of inhabiting the penal settlements of Siberia!

What shall I say of this great city? It is not so beautiful as Munich, but it is the most regularly laid out and solidly built capital of Europe. The streets are wide, and smooth as a house floor. They are scrubbed every morning just as we scrub our halls and porches. Human life is as safe at night as in the day-time. A policeman stands at every crossing. Living here is abundant and cheap. I am spending less money here than I should at home. Wife says that everybody is well dressed except her husband. Our traveling family sleep about nine hours out of every twenty-four. They will be kept wide-awake for the next forty days. We shall get but little rest until we arrive in London next July. Then, for a few days again, we shall test the Neapolitan maxim for all it is worth.

Why do Christians keep their religion so much in abeyance? At the breakfast-table this morning they were telling each other about the concerts, operas, theaters, and what places of *innocent* entertainment would open (free) to-day; but not a word about the location of a church, the hour of service, the music, or the minister. Each person at the table is a member of some Church at home. Finally I called a German maid, who "speaks English a leetle," and inquired for Dr. Stuckenburg's place of worship. In reply she brought the following card: "American and British Union Services, 11:30 A.M., Nos. 5

and 6 Junker Strasse." About one dozen went from our breakfast-table to church. The Doctor is a very learned man, a most impressive preacher. He came to his pulpit just fifteen minutes before there was a sound from the organ. He did not wait, like my St. Louis friend, until the organ "pealed forth," and then march up the aisle with indescribable solemnity. Our preacher to-day wore no robes, read no hymns—did nothing but conduct a plain, extempore service, and preach a pure gospel sermon. No wonder his house is filled every Sunday. His description of "modern society, spending a life-time in the pursuit of trifles—nothings," is equal to any thing Thackeray has written when in his most excoriating moods. Then when he dwelt upon the quiet and peaceable lives of all true Christians, it made me think of Middle Tennessee, and the differences between brethren there who have been life-long friends. That subject never enters my mind without converting my usually delightful wanderings into a *via dolorosa*. Pardon me, dear brethren. A man of my years and present sentiments has nothing to gain or lose by the course of events, but you must allow me, under the influence of the noble utterances I heard to-day, to record my *inexpressible* sorrow.

We shall probably spend our next Lord's day in Warsaw, the ancient capital of Poland, and the next in "Holy Moscow." Fare you well.

Berlin, May 10, 1891.

"HOLY MOSCOW."

IT was easier asked than done. Alex. and I appeared "during office hours," before the Russian Consul-general at Berlin. We spread seven passports before him asking for his *visé*. The dark-haired nobleman looked at us, and we looked at him. He knew no English, we knew no Russian. He sat down, we sat down. There was silence for half an hour. Just then an American lady came in speaking German. So soon as her passport was stamped she became our interpreter. We must first secure the *visé* of Mr. Edwards, the American Consul, and then come to the Russian Consulate. This was done, and we entered the dominions of the Tsar protected by the American eagle and the double-headed black eagle of Russia. This awful-looking, two-headed bird has been doing service since 1472, when Ivan III. married Sophia Palaeologus, daughter of the last Christian Emperor of Constantinople.

Some evening when I am telling the "Tales of a Traveler" I shall give you a description of a company of Laplanders whom I saw before leaving the German capital. There were men, women, and children—fathers, mothers, and *babies*—all clad in furs, from the shores of the Arctic Sea. They exhibited their tents, sledges, implements of labor, cooking-utensils, and scores of other things peculiar to a life spent in the region of perpetual snow and ice. They are a small, white, withered, and tough-looking race. By judicious use of small coins I made several friends among them whom I met frequently afterward. On the same morning I saw some descendants of the Aztecs, from Central America; also an intelligent two-headed, four-armed boy from Italy, and a full-bearded Virginia woman. (I suppose she is a descendant of Esau.)

We left Berlin on Saturday, and came to Breslau to rest and worship on the Lord's day. While listening to the pealing organ and a thousand voices in the Lutheran Church I thought how fortunate it is for Protestantism that the great reformer was so devoted to sacred poetry and music. To the ordinary reader the word "Breslau" seems only a geograpical distinction, yet it designates a flourishing commercial city, about the size of St. Louis, paved and built and covered in as if the workmen intended it to stand forever. And that delightful old German hostelry, *Zum Weissen Adler!* Breslau is the capital of the province of Silesia, to know all about which one must read Carlyle's "Life of Frederick the Great." But in this utilitarian age who cares for the quarrels of "Old Fritz" and Maria Theresa? He lies quietly behind the pulpit in the Garrison Church of Potsdam, and she in a splendid mausoleum in Vienna, and Silesia flourishes as a member of the German Confederacy.

Our next stop was in Warsaw, capital of the ancient kingdom of Poland. We were now in Russia. To know this, we did not have to wait until our arrival at the "Border Station," and the call was made for baggage and passports. In less than a mile after crossing the little brook that divides the two empires, you miss the neat farm-houses, the carefully trimmed hedges, the compact roads, and high cultivation of Eastern Prussia. You enter a country that looks as primitive in every respect as some of our North-western States. About one hundred years ago the various partitions of Poland were completed. The most densely populated portion fell to Austria, the richest part was given to Prussia, while the Russians took the largest area. This included the city of Warsaw. Somebody says: "An emperor, a king, and a Tsar swallowed unhappy Poland without even saying grace." Warsaw is a bright, beautiful, and bustling city of nearly half a million, with stately lines of houses and ample squares. We had only two days to devote to it, but we made good use of them. We drove from 9 in the morning until 8 in the evening. Our *cicerone* was a native born Jew. He knew all the topography, history, and biography, especially the exploits of King John Sobieski and Thaddeus Kosciusko. Wonder if anybody ever lived in Warsaw except those two knightly gentlemen?

Miss Lester was completely obfuscated by the signs. "Well," said she, "this is the first place on our tour where I can neither read nor translate the sign-boards." None of us could assist her.

The long run from Warsaw to Moscow by the way of Minsk, Smolensk, and other well-known cities, gave us some idea of the vastness of the Russian Empire, occupying, as it does, one-seventh part of the land surface of the globe. In 1886 the Tsar and his people numbered only 109,000,000. Any one can see that the country is thinly settled. Forests are always in sight. The inhabitants use wood as we do in America—for building and fencing, and even for fuel. The railroads are the best in the world. At present they measure only 17,000 miles, but others are in course of construction. No trouble to build them: the country is as level as Holland. The *mujiks* (peasants) gather about the railroad stations to see the trains pass. They are dressed very much like the same class of people with us. The *kupets* (traders) look exactly like brisk Yankee merchants. The *boyars* (nobles) are generally in uniform. Everybody is serious. We have not heard a native laugh yet. Every man, woman, and child seems to have an affair to look after. These are robust people.

On reaching Moscow we are in the political and ecclesiastical center of all that is truly Russian. The city is spread over a circumference of twenty-five miles, and has a population of 753,000. Some guide book maker calls it "a vast village." We are at once struck by the busy life in the broad, irregular streets. They are crowded in summer, as well as in winter, with vehicles and pedestrians. High prices rule. No staying at a hotel here on ten *francs* a day; ten *roubles* will pay you through, and leave a few *copeks* over.

Moscow is an old city. Chronicles record its existence more than one thousand years ago. In the year 1862 was celebrated the one thousandth anniversary of the existence of Russia, whether in the form of principalities, independent or confederated, or as the Grand Duchy of Moscow, by which those principalities were absorbed, and ultimately welded into an empire.

Moscow is regarded as a holy city. The Church is every thing here. Hither pilgrims come from all parts of the Russo-Greek world. All Tsars are crowned in Moscow, and each one was buried here up to the time of Peter the Great.

The religion of the eye and the ear, a religion of forms and ceremonies, rarely ever has any effect on the lives of its professors. I had a capital opportunity of proving this to my courier the other day. There is a picture of the Virgin and child, or of some famous saint in the Russian calendar, at every street corner in Moscow. On one of our drives the courier gravely said: " What a religious people these Muscovites are! See how they bow and cross themselves at the corners of the streets!" "Yes," said I, "and the largest building in the city is a foundling hospital, with accommodations for thousands of infants, and it is generally crowded." The four hundred Greek Churches of Moscow, with all their forms and ceremonies, do not seem to have much influence on the *morals* of the men and women. I pray that another word may never be added to the Ritual of our Church, but that several lines may be taken out.

The Grand Duke Sergius, brother of the emperor, is the Governor-general of Moscow. On the day after our arrival, he held a reception in the Kremlin of all the grandees of the city. State carriages by the acre! On the next day he reviewed the troops. If any American wonders how monarchy is maintained in the Old World, he should see more than twenty acres of well-drilled officers and soldiers. The standing army of Russia numbers 1,000,000.

We remained about a week in "Moscow the white walled." Of course we saw the Romanoff House, the Petrofski Palace and Park, all the wonders and untold wealth of the Kremlin, the gorgeous churches, lofty towers, big bells, and ancient mausoleums. But all these will make a good theme for another lecture, and I must print no more at present.

We have plenty of light in this country. The sun was up at 3 o'clock this morning. It is now 10 o'clock at night, and not dark yet. I shall have to get my people out of Russia on account of the heat. I shall date this letter May 25, but all the papers this morning are dated May 13. "Old Style" is twelve days later than "New Style." Do you understand? Ask Dr. Garland.

May 25, 1891.

THE RUSSIAN CAPITAL.

WE left Moscow on the 26th of May, and arrived at St. Petersburg the next day. We passed the imperial train at night. The Tsar was going to Moscow to celebrate the tenth anniversary of his coronation. Every mile of the road was guarded by soldiers. "Seeing is believing." The encampments were about five miles apart. The Russian officers and soldiers wear gray coats. They look like they would fight.

The railroad from Moscow to St. Petersburg is so perfectly balanced, and the compartments of the train are so admirably arranged, that one can hold a quiet and satisfactory conversation, or sleep soundly. The second-class cars are better than first-class in Spain or Italy. The conductors, or guards, are always ready to say and do pleasant things. I could entertain you, or harrow you up, with an account of the arrest of Nihilists, the departure of exiles to Siberia, and the exodus of Jews, but everybody knows that I prefer the bright side of things. So I must record the cleanliness and comfort of railroad traveling and the politeness and accommodation of hotel functionaries. Hotel life is a luxury in Russia. I am now writing in a room of Hotel de France nearly as large and comfortable as the "living room" of Alexander II. in the Winter Palace. (Wife and the young people are taking an evening drive by *daylight* at 10 o'clock P.M. If I go down for coffee to-morrow morning at 7, I shall probably find the servants scrubbing up the dining-room.)

Moscow, the ancient capital, is in the heart of European Russia. Peter the Great grew tired of the place in 1703, and resolved to have a "window looking out into Europe." So he built himself a cabin in a low swamp, just where the river Neva empties into the Gulf of Finland. That is where St. Petersburg now stands. At a distance it looks like the city is floating, but it is well pegged down to the moist crust of the earth. Every house, even the vast cathedral of St. Isaacs, is built on piles twenty-one feet long. The place overflows, but it has not washed away yet. "*Après nous le déluge.*"

St. Petersburg contains one million of inhabitants, and is built upon a scale of vastness and magnificence far superior to any modern capital. It is like the Russian empire—immense; but not so monotonous. The Landaus and *proliotkis*, drawn by superb horses, are flying in all directions. They move at run-away speed, and among their drivers we find ethnographical types on which we gaze with the interest we would bestow on a Hindoo or a Chinaman in London. Their dress is almost a mediæval survival of long, coarse, blue robes; and the head-dress is clearly a modernized descendant of the "beef-eater's" hat, brought to Russia by the adventurous Englishman, who discovered the sea-board of Muscovy in the sixteenth century.

There is busy, noisy life in the market-houses as well as on the streets. These are huge inclosures, with avenues and stalls laid off with perfect regularity, and they are kept clean. The people who sell and those who buy are dressed very much like the same classes of people in our own country. We have never heard of any thing to eat that may not be found in a St. Petersburg market-place.

The palace of Louis XIV., at Versailles, has always been our example and illustration of the utmost regal splendor; but in every thing except building material and architecture it must now take second rank. An absolute monarchy surpasses all others in the erection of colossal edifices and the collection of costly furniture and adornments, simply from the fact that there is nothing like a legislative body to vote for or against a budget of expenses. Bear witness the temples and tombs of Egypt, the palaces on the Bosporus at Constantinople, and those of Moscow and St. Petersburg. The fiats of Pharaohs, Sultans, and Tsars have been sufficient for any undertaking. We left Moscow thinking that half the wealth of the world, invested in royal goods, in robes, crowns, jewels, plate, armor, carriages, thrones, and the like, had been stored in the Kremlin (fortress); but we come to the capital to find every thing duplicated and even surpassed.

The Winter Palace on the "Great Square" was completed in 1769 by Catharine the Great. This immense edifice may be considered as emblematical of the magnitude of the empire, and of the power by which it is governed and held together. Connected with the palace, but entered by a noble vestibule from without, is the famed Hermitage, originally the Pavilion, built in 1765, in which the great Catharine spent her leisure moments with philosophers, men of letters, and artists. Among the ten thousand of other books may be found remnants of the libraries of Voltaire, D'Alembert, and Diderot. We spent the best part of two days in the Winter Palace and the Hermitage. At the close, when we were all exhausted, one of the young people inquired how many miles we had walked. The question was not inappropriate. This royal abode, besides others in the city and suburbs, is a wonderful improvement on "Peter's House" at the mouth of the Neva, and Peterhof, many miles out on the shores of the Gulf of Finland, both of which we visited yesterday.

The interior of St. Isaacs, the cathedral of St. Petersburg, is well calculated to inspire feelings of solemnity and veneration. As in all Russo-Greek churches, the purposely subdued light brings into relief the glittering sumptuousness of the *ikonostas*, or screen, and of the *ikons*, mostly in mosaic work, which adorn the walls and pillars of the temple. Theologians of the Greek Church say that these are not worshiped. To my mind, the belief in images, to which miraculous powers are ascribed, is not easily distinguishable from actual material adoration. The Russo-Greek Church rejects as idolatrous any carved or molded representation of saintly or sacred subjects for purposes of worship; but holds that an *ikon* painted or produced in Mosaic work, on a flat surface, is not a violation of the Second Commandment.

We attended service at St. Isaacs on the anniversary of the coronation of the present emperor, and heard the Te Deum sung, and on several other occasions. At the Kasan Cathedral we saw an infant baptized by trine immersion. There are many costly votive objects and military trophies in this Cathedral, and the emperor never fails to offer up his prayers here immediately on his departure from the capital and his return after a residence at some other imperial seat. Peter the Great and all the emperors since his day lie buried in the Cathedral of St. Peter and St. Paul, within the fortress.

We have just returned from the Imperial Public Library. It is the largest library in the world but one. The number of printed volumes is over one million, and that of manuscripts about thirty-four thousand. In addition, there are eighty thousand engravings and maps. In one room are all the different pictures of Peter the Great ever made. I once saw, at Stratford-upon-Avon, all the pictures of Washington Irving. Peter ranks him. The *Ostromir* manuscript in the old

Slavonic character, and containing the Evangelistarium, bears the date of 1056—that is, it was written about seventy years after the introduction of Christianity into Russia. A Greek *codex* of the four Evangelists, on parchment black with age, bears proof of its having been written in the ninth century. A copy of the Koran, made by a caliph of the ninth century, is also on exhibition. A still older manuscript, the chief glory of this department, is the famous *Codex Sinaiticus*, a complete copy of the Greek Bible, written in the fourth century, and discovered by Tischendorf in the Convent of St. Catharine, on Mount Sinai, in 1859. Those who suppose the Russians know nothing of the opinions entertained of them by other nations should see a room in this library, containing thirty thousand volumes in all languages (except Russian) that relate to the geography, history, and government of the empire.

There is a reading-room in this hotel, where native and foreign newspapers and magazines are free to all the guests. The English publications, especially the *Times* and the *Standard*, just teem with editorials and dispatches animadverting upon the government of Russia, and denouncing it for its opposition to the Jewish race. From these and other sources the Russians can learn all about themselves. The Jews are also taught the cause of their troubles.

It is known to all that the late emperor was assassinated by the Nihilists. The other day, under the direction of an old guide, I saw the place where he lunched on that fatal day, the spot where the bombs exploded, the carriage that was shivered to splinters, and the bed on which he died. This was Tsar Alexander II., the one who emancipated over eighty millions of serfs.

We leave here to-morrow for Finland, that country never visited by American tourists. My next letter may be from "The Land of a Thousand Lakes," or "The Lake of a Thousand Isles," as Finland is called by her loving sons.

St. Petersburg, June 1, 1891.

NORTH OF THE BALTIC SEA.

AFTER a long journey we are in London for the mid-summer. We left St. Petersburg with the following sentences formulating: It takes humanity a long while to become human. After all our boasting about the brotherhood of Christianized people, we frequently find men barbarians at heart. The present attitude of the Russian Government toward millions of Jews is in conflict with the civilization of the 19th century, and against the universal conscience of mankind. There are facts in connection with this subject that I should scarcely require an American audience to believe, and yet I propose to tell them when I get home. All that George Kennan has said concerning the penal settlements in Siberia may be surpassed by the story of the cruelties now practiced upon multitudes of offending and unoffending Jews.

> Tribes of the wandering foot and weary breast,
> Where shall ye flee away and be at rest?
> The wild bird hath his nest, the fox his cave,
> Mankind their country, but Israel the grave.

Most tourists prefer the water route from St. Petersburg—sailing down the Gulf of Finland, and across the Gulf of Bothnia to the Swedish capital. We came "down to our work," and took the land route, crossing Finland from side to side at the widest part. The country is seven hundred miles from North to South, and two hundred miles from East to West. The population numbers a little over two millions, 85 per cent. of whom are peasants.

Every thing looks extremely Northern. The soil is thin, and all that grows out of it is stunted or dwarfed. The people have fair complexions, light hair, and heavy garments. Everybody appears to be serious, sober, and industrious in this well-ordered and much-governed country. It would be considered a rare thing to find a man or a woman in Finland who cannot read and write. They all belong to the Lutheran Church, and outside of the towns and villages there are thousands of them who walk many miles to the "meeting-house."

There are some Americans who would enjoy the free and easy manners of the railroad eating-houses of Finland. We went in, called for a table, and sat down, expecting to be served by the usual waiters. Nobody paid any attention to us, and there we sat. Directly we noticed a very large table in the middle of the room, loaded with bread, meat, vegetables, sweets, and the like. Every one who came in picked up a plate, knife and fork, walked up to this table, and helped himself. Our hungry girls were not backward in going forward. So we fared sumptuously. When the meal was finished, each passenger hunted up the cashier of the establishment, handed him a marc and a half, and passed out to the train. Everybody took his time for every thing. "Never hurry except when catching fleas," is the motto of Finland. Viborg is the shipping port of the country. The place contains 17,000 inhabitants. We stopped there long enough to see a castle that was built in 1293. Nothing interests the average tourist more than a shattered old pile of the middle ages.

Helsingfors has been the capital of the Grand Duchy since 1819, the seat of a university since 1827, and owes much of its prosperity to the political connection of Finland with Russia. It is a grand little city of 23,-000, and the presence of 100 professors and 1,700 students reminds one of Cambridge. The hotels are exceptionally fine.

We had no business in Abo except to see the Cathedral of St. Henry, with its rude and heavy Gothic exterior. The first Episcopal chair of Finland was instituted within its walls after their consecration by Bishop Magnus in A.D. 1300, when the city itself was removed to its present site from its pagan foundations a short distance up the river. This "old city" was founded A.D. 1157. Abo has 23,000 inhabitants, and was the seat of a great university up to the fire of 1827.

In 1809 Sweden ceded to Russia all her rights over Finland, and after a separate negotiation between the Finnish Diet and Alexander I. the Estates swore allegiance to the Tsar as the Grand Duke of Finland. The maintenance of the Lutheran religion and the integrity of their Constitution, together with all previous rights and privileges, were assured to the Finlanders in a solemn manifesto which continues to this day to be their zealously guarded Charter of Rights. In virtue of it they have a Diet of their own, composed of four estates—nobles, clergy, burgesses, and peasantry.

In regard to religion and education, the Finlanders have reason to be proud of the results of the legacy bequeathed to them by their old Scandinavian masters. An excellent system of instruction is zealously carried out under the superintendency of the Lutheran clergy, who do not admit to the communion any person who is unable to read or write.

We rounded out from Abo in the midst of a furious snow-storm, June 4. This troubled the waters of the Gulf of Bothnia, and we all lost reputation as sailors, except Alex. The boy is getting to be a regular "old sea-dog."

We are comfortably quartered in London at an inn where we have stopped twice before. At the table adjoining ours we have the company of a friend of my boyhood—Zeb Vance, of North Carolina. He and I parted at Washington College forty-five years ago. With no introduction or hesitancy we shook hands instantly. We are both getting old, fleshy, and gray. How did we know each other at this distance of time and place? Senator Vance is accompanied by his wife and son. In the evening he sent up the following card:

Dear Young: If not too late when you come in, let me know, and meet me in the ladies' drawing-room for a *talk*. VANCE.

We did not talk about ourselves, but of the boys we knew long ago—of their history, successes, defeats, death. Then we spoke of the changes in religious history and worship. At the close of this conversation, he looked me earnestly in the face and said: "Young, you have read the history of the Church and have *now* seen modern Christianity in all its phases. Is not our good old country meeting-house worship the purest and best?" To which I replied with emphasis: "*It is.*" And then I delivered my mind on every species of Ritualism. That is the germ and cause of all the evils that have crept into our beautiful and holy religion.

We were wandering through Westminster Abbey the other day, when we had the pleasure of meeting Col. Ed Baxter, wife, and daughter, of Nashville; also Mr. Ben Allen and wife. It is difficult to express the delight one feels when he sees the face of a compatriot in a strange land. I told them that there were twenty-two Nashville people over in Paris. When I asked Col. Baxter how he found time to leave home, he answered: "I just pulled away." There are other hard-wrought people who ought to pull away. "But it costs so much money!" All right, old gentlemen! Stick to your slavery. Make secure investments. Watch them closely. Live in hope. Your sons-in-law will be along after awhile.

London, June 26, 1891.

STILL DUE NORTH.

AFTER a miserable night on the Gulf of Bothnia, we landed at the Swedish capital. In every respect the approach to Stockholm surpasses that to Constantinople. Nature and art have left nothing undone to charm the eye and excite the admiration of a stranger. If any hotel in Europe surpasses "The Grand Hotel" here, we have not been fortunate enough to unpack within its walls.

Stockholm has been the capital of Sweden for six hundred years. It is called "the Venice of the North," because it is built on islands. However, the islands are larger than those on which the Italian Venice is built. It has, perhaps, a population of 200,000, and the architecture of the place is as solid as Edinburgh. We were taken to the top of the celebrated "Lift," where we had a bird's-eye view of the city and its environs. Then we drove all over the place. The "Museums of Northern Antiquities" here would interest any man of sense or sensibility. The palace, built on an island, is large, massive, plain; and the occupant, Oscar II., is the third king of the Bernadotte family. They say that he is the tallest man in Europe. (I am off the continent now.)

While wife and the young ladies were taking their ease at their inn, Alex. and I made the excursion to Upsala. This is the historical, intellectual, and religious center of Sweden. It is the charmed spot, the enchanted ground, of the kingdom; for here the old kings and vikings lived and stormed and died; here Christianity was introduced, more than fifteen hundred years ago, and paganism fought its last battle with the new faith; here the great university was founded, and here it still grows and flourishes.

The road to Upsala extends due north along the coast. On our arrival a turn-out was offered us, in which we made the circuit of the little city. We found it clean and cold. An archbishop resides here, whose church is the grandest brick structure we have seen. The university buildings are plain and enormous. The great treasure of the library is the "*Codex Argentius*." It is a translation of the four Gospels, made by Bishop Ulphilas in the fourth century. The manuscript contains 188 leaves, written in silver and gold. The language is Moeso-Gothic, the only specimen of that language now in the world.

In the afternoon we drove to Gamla, Upsala. There is nothing left here except four huge mounds and an ancient stone church. On these mounds were performed the bloody rites of the old Scandinavian religion. The largest is named Woden; the next Thor; the third Freya; and the fourth is called the Assize Hill. From the top of this the pagan kings addressed the multitude below and issued their proclamations. (There was no printing in those days.) The church-building marks the spot where Christianity was introduced. When, the next day, I saw in Stockholm the glitter of the gorgeous vestments of the Lutheran clergy and the performance of an elaborate ritual, I thought of the simple worship that must have been offered in this venerable pile. The rites of Gothic heathenism have gone out, but forms and ceremonies borrowed from the mythology of Greece and Rome have come in. All hierarchy and ritualism point to one result: the ruin of the Church as a means of converting men to the religion taught in the New Testament. The magnet does not lie.

It does not take one long to learn who are the demi-gods of Swedish history: Queen Margaret, Gustavus Vasa, Gustavus Adolphus, Charles XII., and Marshal Bernadotte. Their pictures and statues are everywhere.

The Swedes are refined, kind-hearted, polite. A gentleman does not enter even a shop without taking off his hat. Since leaving New York I have not slept without folding my coat, containing letter of credit, under my head. In Sweden I retired as if I were at home.

Now let us turn our attention to London. Yesterday was Sunday. For months I have been witnessing the idolatrous ceremonials of the Romish Church in France, Spain, and

Italy, and the gorgeous rites of the Greek Church in Poland and Russia. Of course my soul longed—"yea, even fainted"—for some court of the Lord, where I could enjoy an extemporaneous, intellectual, and spiritual service. So, as Mr. Spurgeon is not well, I went to hear Joseph Parker. A Wesleyan preacher can state the plan of salvation as well as any man in the world, but he must needs wear a robe and spend the first hour in reading the Morning Service of the Church of England before "he takes his text." I am tired of the rags (gowns) of popery. I am weary of written prayers. Dr. Parker, in his suit of black, with black cravat and turn-down collar, and with his manly and mighty utterance of the pure gospel, suits me exactly. I would exchange him for our own Bishop Wilson, but my dear and beloved friend was not here to preach. Wilson's head reminds me of the Greenwich Observatory: it is so solid that it never jostles or trembles. He says and seals, but his heart is as tender as a mother's before he says it.

Mr. Spurgeon is very sick with the prevailing influenza. His people believe in the religion he has taught them. An all-day prayer-meeting was announced yesterday. At 7 o'clock this morning they met in the Tabernacle, and have been praying ever since for the recovery of their pastor. "It shall not be said that praying breath was ever spent in vain."

I know nothing of Church affairs at home. Two papers should have been mailed to me regularly, but they have not come. My friends are beginning to write, but the most of their letters ask for lectures. A few of these shall be delivered in aid of Church enterprises, for which I have always worked. A *tempting* invitation from a Lecture Bureau in New York City has also been received. I shall answer "No," because I prefer my old manner of life.

The young Emperor of Germany, a grandson of Victoria, is expected here this week. He has mentioned one of two Sundays in July when he will be pleased to visit the Royal Naval Exhibition. As soon as this took air, a member of the House of Commons called the attention of the British Parliament to the proposition, asking the royal gentleman to appoint another day. A note of animadversion also rang out from the most robust of the city pulpits last Sunday. Another day has been named. England is not Germany, thank the Lord. England keeps holy the Sabbath-day.

All Russia shudders from sea to sea. The crop report for June, published by the Minister of Finance, shows that a famine is inevitable—such a famine as the Tsar and his people have not experienced since the Romanoffs have been on the throne. To avert the calamity, the priests are *reading* prayers to the Lord from every altar in the empire and sprinkling every acre of the reluctant soil with holy water. It may be that the Lord is turning their attention away from the unfortunate Jews.

My near neighbors, Mrs. Burch and her son, have just arrived. Miss Seawell and her traveling party are in town. Maj. Stahlman and family left for Paris this morning. We have bought our return tickets, and shall be at home about the 1st of September. Somebody may ask if our wanderings will then come to an end. I do not know.

London, June 30, 1891.

TOWARD THE MIDNIGHT SUN.

THE entire kingdom of Norway, with eleven hundred miles of sea-coast, does not contain more people than the single city of London; but they are the simplest, cleanest, and most religious people we ever saw outside of our own Southland.

The water approach to Christiania is equal to that of Stockholm. The present capital of Norway was founded in 1624. It has now a population approaching 100,000. The former capital was Bergen. The ancient capital was Throndhjem. We visited them all before leaving the cold and sterile region. We did not see the "Midnight Sun;" but we saw it shining one hour before midnight, and that explained the whole cosmic wonder.

Norway once depended upon Copenhagen for the education of her sons, but she now has a university of her own, situated in the center of Christiania, numbering fifty professors and one thousand students. Most of the museums and scientific collections of the city are on the university grounds. Here also we saw the famous Viking Ship, seventy-six feet in length by sixteen feet in breadth. When an old Norse Viking died, a vast excavation was made in the earth, where his ship and himself, his horse and all his implements of warfare were buried. This one at Christiania was dug up on the shore of a Fjord on the Southern coast. "What folly!" exclaims the reader. Please take notice, my friend, that if the Archbishop of Canterbury were to die to-day, the Londoners would bury him in his robes and miter, and with all the insignia of his high office. The Archbishop is probably a descendant of the old Viking, but the race has been churched and civilized, rolled and combed and perfumed a great deal since then.

After driving over the city, and wandering through the Deserted Palace, we spent the evening in the Norwegian Parliament. Sweden and Norway are both under one crown, but each has its own legislative body. The Norse Parliament is composed of an Upper House and a Lower House. The first is called the Lagthing, the second the Storthing. We visited the Lower House. The members were elegantly dressed, and the presiding officer had them well in hand. Each member spoke from a manuscript. So you may know the proceedings were orderly and dull. Whenever the manuscript comes in, bid farewell to eloquence and excitement. "Drowsy tinklings lull the distant folds." Manufactures are in great esteem over here —manufactured orthodoxies, liturgies, sermons, speeches, and proceedings.

From Christiania to Throndhjem seemed a great distance to us, but we made the journey in a little over four days. The first day by rail and steamer to Lillehamar was easy enough. The last three by carioles ought to have worn us out completely. To drive two hundred miles in three days keeps one busy, especially if he eats three meals a day, and sleeps at a way-side inn at night. Moreover, we changed carioles and horses six or seven times a day. Each fresh little Norwegian trotter seemed wilder than the one we had left behind. The people of the country do not understand a word you say; but when you drive up to one "station," they fit you out immediately for the next. A cariole holds only one person, and he does his own driving. We are bringing a sketch model home, in the hope that some enterprising carriage-maker will introduce the vehicle.

Throndhjem is the largest city in the world so far north as the latitude of Iceland. It contains about 25,000 souls. Most of the houses are built of wood, like those of Abo, in Finland. The streets are broad, and the open spaces, or squares, are large. This plan was adopted in view of the danger from conflagrations.

All Norwegian history centers in Throndhjem. So of literature and religion. The Cathedral of St. Olaf is the oldest and largest place of worship in all Scandinavia. It is considered so sacred that the Constitution of the country requires all kings to be crowned here. The government of the country has appropriated 80,000 crowns a year for its restoration. According to the calculations of the architect, these repairs extend from 1869 to 1925. We attended service twice on Sunday. There are no forms or ceremonies. The service was as simple and impressive as a venerable Lutheran minister could make it. This accounts for the piety of the people.

We went so far north that we could see to read good print at any hour of the night. On the 21st of June the sun dips under the horizon at 11 o'clock, and comes up again at 1 o'clock. The absence of fruits and the abundance of all meats indicated that we were among people who live near the frigid zone.

Norway is the wildest country we have seen except Switzerland, but the roads are perfect. The drives to the various waterfalls in the neighborhood of Throndhjem are as delightful as one could ask.

A sail of two days and nights down the western coast of Norway brought us to Bergen. It was a very quiet and pleasant run, for the numerous islands along the coast shelter the water. The hotels of Bergen are superb. They live on tourists. The drives of the back country are generally lined with travelers.

Then we came across the North Sea in the good ship "Britannia." She is a monster that behaves beautifully among the waves. When we approached Newcastle, we found the fog so dense that it required us nearly all day to land. Strange that one cannot approach England without getting befogged! We did finally get ashore, and slept that night in the stately city of Edinburgh. After a little rest in the Scottish capital, and revisiting the famous spots, we journeyed south to see some English country life. But all roads lead to London.

The most unique collection we have seen is the Royal Naval Exhibition at Chelsea. Whatever relates to the study of oceans and seas, ship building and navigation, is here. Pictures of naval heroes, sea fights and victories, are in abundance. Lord Nelson is the demi-god, and Trafalgar the greatest victory ever won on water. So the English think. But for their experience with the Thirteen Colonies, I suppose they would be tempted to take the word "surrender" out of the dictionary. Patriotism is a prominent virtue. They sing "God Save the Queen" in Canon Farrar's Church. Paganism is still a pew-holder.

Dr. Parker preaches a sermon every Thursday at 12 o'clock in the City Temple, and has been doing so for twenty-two years. His church is packed every time. A glance at the heads of the men last Thursday reminded one of a convention of bankers. They did not sing a national hymn, but they did sing "What a friend we have in Jesus!" Dr. Parker has driven paganism out of his Church. Christ reigns there. Glory be to his name forever!

How rapidly time flies! So every old man thinks. Here now is another Fourth of July. I am going to see the American flag before night. "Long may it wave!" It points to the freest and happiest country the world ever saw. I beg pardon for referring to age. Christians ought to feel young as they approach that blessed immortality where they publish no almanacs.

London, July 4, 1891.

LONDON DAY BY DAY.

ON the first Sunday in July we attended the Wesleyan Chapel on Great Queen Street. We timed the "Morning Service of the Church of England," as it was read and sung from the "Book of Common Prayer." It lasted exactly one hour. The preacher stood on his feet, and even leaned backward occasionally, during these *devotional* exercises. We never heard this service so well done before. The preacher and people read and sung with genuine Methodist vigor and solemnity. The sermon was short, well delivered, and full of meaning. If the Rev. George Kenyon should ever see this paragraph, I suggest to him that John Wesley and the early Methodists knelt when they prayed. In the afternoon we were present at a revival meeting held in Exeter Hall. The evangelist was a Methodist from our own country. No man ever stated the plan of salvation more clearly. If he had only left out the usual interesting (?) allusions to himself and his achievements, the sermon would have been worthy of Spurgeon. The evening service found us at the City Temple again. Parker gets better and better.

The Salvation Army celebrated their 26th anniversary on Monday night. The great audience-room at Exeter Hall was crowded at one shilling admittance fee. With martial music, waving flags, and storms of applause, "General" Booth was received on the platform. He is an old gentleman (with an immense beard), who puts on quiet airs, and seems cool as a statue in the midst of his noisy and enthusiastic followers. There were present on the platform, in their national costume, no less than one hundred and twenty "officers" (preachers) from foreign lands. I must say their hymns and prayers and speeches were strictly evangelical. The fanatical creatures all seemed to have learned the exact way of salvation: Repentance, faith in Christ, love to Christ, obedience to Christ. The speakers were from England,

America, Germany, Finland, Italy, Australia, Norway, and Zululand. Somehow, somewhere, somewhen, they had all learned enough of English to express themselves. Is not our language the best vehicle for the conveyance of gospel truth to all nations? These "Salvationists" publish, in books, magazines, and weekly papers, quite a voluminous literature. We left before the meeting closed. From all serious things that are not done "decently and in order," good Lord deliver us! A gentleman is quiet, a lady is serene. Bishop McTyeire could "do things," bring events to pass, accomplish great results, and keep cool about it. He seemed to have no "energy"—broke no double-trees or single-trees—but he invariably moved his load. Bishop Wilson is his nearest of kin.

We spent the afternoon of Tuesday at City Road Chapel and in Bunhill Fields Cemetery. They are "restoring" the old cradle of Methodism. Contributions of costly materials are coming from some other parts of the world. They showed us a marble column from America. The workmen leave Wesley's house just as it stood when he died. What a pity the old chapel has been made to look so modern! After visiting the tombs of John Wesley, Adam Clarke, Joseph Benson, and others, we stepped across the street into Bunhill Fields. There sleep John Bunyan, Isaac Watts, Daniel Defoe, Susanna Wesley, and many more.

London has seven months of winter, and five months of bad weather. The rain was pouring so profusely on Wednesday morning that we could make no excursions above ground, so we concluded to take a long ride on the Metropolitan Under-ground railway. We found the road a model of excellence, and the trains superb. It was a little darker than usual as we passed under the river Thames. We are all on *terra firma* now, and the girls are spending a delightful afternoon shopping.

It is scarcely necessary to mention the fact that the German Emperor is making a ten days' visit to his grandmother, Queen Victoria. I suppose the American papers are teeming with dispatches concerning his "progress." Each morning paper here devotes columns to it, informing the public how and when every step is taken. He landed at Windsor Castle on Saturday, attended a Thanksgiving service on Sunday, was present at a royal marriage on Monday, received a State banquet on Tuesday, came to the city on Wednesday, is holding a drawing-room at Buckingham Palace to-day, will attend the Italian opera to-night, will make a procession through the city to-morrow and attend another banquet, will visit the Royal Naval Exhibition on Saturday, attend church on Sunday, and so on. This is the merest outline of the programme. Walks, rides, drives, reviews, luncheons, and garden parties fill in. The young Emperor has always been remarkable for his unflagging industry and untiring attention to business. Since he came to the throne all Europe has been astonished at the revelation of his ability. Instead of Bismarck, he keeps *himself* before the public. In times of peace he proposes to command the ship of State; and if war should come, he holds himself ready to lead his army. This is what the German peoples have always admired. It is rather interesting to notice the comparisons that are made, or rather the contrasts drawn, between the Emperor and his uncle, the Prince of Wales. (Since writing this paragraph I have read the morning papers. The young Kaiser has broken out in so many new and unexpected places that my gossiping pencil reluctates. He has received a delegation and an address from the fishmongers.)

All Thursday has been consumed by a visit to the Kew Gardens. We tried the Under-ground railway again. Our young friend from Nashville, J. Sykes Gilbert, accompanied us. Mr. George Dazey and his partner, Mr. Dobbins, are also on this side. Landscape gardening has displayed all its science and art in the Kew Gardens. After six days of constant seeing and hearing in the great city, it is restful and refining to pass a whole day in such a place as Kew.

Our last journey from London was made to Windsor Castle, Eton College, and Stoke Pogis Church. The English people submit to the expense of keeping a number of palaces to shelter their royal family. I mention the following: St. James, Buckingham, Windsor, Balmoral, Osborne, Hampton Court, Marlborough House, Sandringham, and how many more?

Mr. Spurgeon seems to be nearing his end. Was there ever such a sensation produced by the illness of a city pastor? Each morning paper contains a "bulletin" from his physicians announcing how he passed the night. Messages of sympathy are wired from all parts of the Christian world. The Primate of the Church of England has visited him. The Archdeacon of London has eulogized him in a sermon from the pulpit of St. Paul's Cathedral.

The London "Season" is now over, and the great event of the season a thing of the past. Of course I refer to the *public reception* of the German Emperor at Guildhall. The city has always been generous in its welcome to foreign sovereigns. The Sultan of Turkey is welcomed one year, the Shah of Persia another; now it is the Emperor of the French who is received, and then the King of Sardinia; the Imperial Tsar is entertained, and so is the Emperor of Brazil. Nor do these people limit their welcome to the illustrious personages whose stately names are inscribed in the *Almanach de Gotha*. Men not very far advanced in years can recollect the welcome given by London to Louis Kossuth, and later still to Garibaldi. This city has, more than once, even in our own days, entertained reigning sovereigns, who afterward came back to be received with courtesy as imperial or royal exiles. And if the President of the French Republic should visit England, he would be received by the city of London with as much cordiality as could be shown to any king or kaiser. The streets of the city, which have echoed for centuries to the tread of royal processions, would witness a monster demonstration in honor of M. Carnot.

The great preachers of London may be counted on one's fingers. Parker is the most intellectual, Spurgeon is the most eloquent, Farrar the most rhetorical, Newman

Hall the most religious. We chose Hall this morning, and were amply repaid. The old gentleman is seventy-five years of age. He offered his resignation last week.

The English boast that the music of St. Paul's is the finest in Europe. They have fought and colonized around the world. They have grasped every inch of soil and sand within their reach. They can digest more heavy meat and swallow more strong drink than any nation on earth. From the days of William the Conqueror they have tolerated wicked rulers enough to curse the world. But the English are neither artists nor musicians. The singing we heard at St. Paul's this afternoon is not to be compared with that of the Russo-Greek Church, nor is it to be named alongside the *Miserere* of Italy. Their public speakers, with a few exceptions, would not be heard a second time by an American audience; but they can build engines, grind steel, spin cotton, weave cloth, train scholars, write books, make laws, and shatter to pieces half the navies of the world.

This evening we went around to the Wesleyan Chapel and heard an excellent sermon. American tourists are returning in such numbers that we expect a crowded ship. Good-night! Look for us August 20.

London, July 13, 1891.

PARIS DAY BY DAY.

THE day before we left London, a correspondent telegraphed us not to reach Paris on Tuesday evening. The people would be celebrating the 14th of July, and not a vehicle would be allowed on the streets after sundown. But we came on, not at all averse to witnessing a "Fete" that marks the day when the Bastile was destroyed, 102 years ago. The English Channel was as "smooth as a dollar," and the journey from London to Paris was uneventful. On our arrival three cabmen offered to take us, by a roundabout way, to Hotel St. Petersburg. We found our rooms all ready.

This place seems to be the paradise of Americans. We have met twenty-two Nashvillians already. Our good friends, B. F. Wilson and family, Miss Seawell and her company, Harry Evans and his bridal party, are among the number. Wilson reads *The American* and sends it around.

The Paris papers each day announce the state of Mr. Spurgeon's health. All ranks and classes of people have paid their respects to him—princes, nobles, statesmen, prelates, preachers, and scholars. Telegrams of sympathy arrive daily from all parts of the world. Mr. Gladstone's letter is the best I have seen. Was ever a city pastor so popular and so beloved?

Some years ago I read "The Augustan Age of France." It was one of the most interesting works of pure literature that I have seen. Pascal opened the literary glories of the reign of Louis XIV.; Fenelon, Molière, Racine, and others came later. To-day has been spent among their monuments. That to Pascal is the tallest. Several of the others may be found in Père la Chaise Cemetery.

In this city of the dead one pauses at many a spot. Here lie Abelard and Heloise; and although they have been dead five hundred years, fresh and costly bouquets are laid on their tombs every day. Who places the flowers there? No one seems to know. Like

Swift and Stella in Dublin, these erring and sinful lovers lie side by side. An iron railing incloses the large space allotted to them, and they sleep under a marble canopy. Evergreens and roses are planted all around. The grave of Marshal Ney is beautifully ornamented, but no monument has been erected. The mausoleum of President Theirs is the most pretentious structure in this celebrated burial-place. If any one wishes to know how wickedly a great Frenchman can live, let him question me about M. Theirs.

The Chicago World's Fair Commissioners have arrived in Paris. Their names are Mr. William Lindsley, Mr. A. G. Bullock, Herr Butterworth, Herr Handy, and Herr Peck. The Germans in London sent an influential deputation to the Victoria Station to see them off. Notice the number of "Herrs." No one will be surprised. In Chicago, which has a population of 1,000,000, there are 400,-000 Germans. The great majority of the public offices of that city are in their hands. There are more "Sangerbunds" and German beer saloons in Chicago than there are lampposts. It thus follows that the decision to make the World's Fair primarily a German Exhibit is hailed with immense delight over in Fatherland. "So *Galignani* says."

If I were an ethnologist, I should like to visit Paris next year. Steps have been taken by the committee appointed for that purpose to organize the Exhibition of the Human Races to take place in 1892. M. de Quatrefages, member of the Institute, is, of course, at the head of the committee. He has already received the promise of several distinguished explorers to bring to Paris types of all the principal races from different parts of the world. Each group of individuals will be provided with all the tools employed for their work, and for the construction of their dwellings, which they will themselves build on the ground to be allotted to them. This arrangement will permit them to pass their time in their customary manner, and thus enable the visitors to learn much of their manners and customs.

The final results of the French census of 1891 are now known. The entire population of France on April 12 of the present year amounted to 38,095,150, being an increase of 208,584 over the census of 1886. Seven cities like London could furnish as many souls as all the French Republic.

Regularly every Sunday we attend the Wesleyan Methodist Church. There is less paganism here ("vain repetitions") than we find in any other Church of the city. But after the eulogy to-day on "Old John Brown" and Henry Ward Beecher, I am not prepared to say where we shall worship next Sunday. The preacher even rehearsed some lines of that miserable doggerel concerning "John Brown's body." Had Bishop Keener been present, he would have been tempted to "speak in meeting." I know his aversion to that song.

This letter is not written to chronicle our daily routine as sight-seers, or to describe the delightful excursions to the environs of Paris. I attended to all this when I was here in the fall of 1886, and again in the summer of 1887. See "Twenty Thousand Miles." (The edition of that book ordered by Thomas Cook & Son, of London, is exhausted.)

The mailing clerk of the Publishing House sent me a package of *Christian Advocates* containing my published letters. I am sorry to infer that so many of them have been lost. These shall be reproduced, and more shall be written, when I publish "Sketchy Pages of European Travel."

The authorities of the Epworth League were kind enough to ask me to write a Church History for young people—a book of 312 pages. For this the material has been collected.

During the solitary hours which I frequently enjoy in Paris, I read the New Testament with an interest and delight never experienced before. I must write a little book to be called "Introduction to the Study of the New Testament." There are some "notions" in the religious world that are not taught in that sacred volume. Adieu!

Paris, July 27, 1891.

FAREWELL TO FRANCE.

WE are not of those who believe that Paris is France; so before leaving the beautiful and bad city, we made some excursions to the country. Matthew Arnold wrote an essay to prove that the French peasantry are the most industrious and prosperous in the world.

Our first trip was to Versailles. Thirty-two Americans found comfortable seats in a carriage drawn by six horses. At certain places on the route, our courier would order a halt, and give us a lecture in tolerable English. Here are a few of his statements made in the course of the day:

The church of St. Augustine was erected to commemorate the birth of the Prince Imperial, son of Napoleon III. This prince was the young fellow who was captured and slain in Zululand.

The favorite resort of Parisians, Bois de

Boulogne, was originally a game preserve, but is now a public park, under the control of a municipality. It covers 2,250 acres—less than Phœnix Park, Dublin; larger than Hyde Park, London; inferior to Central Park, New York.

The English and American visitor will be shocked to find that all through the spring and autumn races are run at Longchamps nearly every Sunday afternoon. There is, however, none of the rowdyism which prevails on the English turf, while the charge of an admission fee contributes greatly to exclude disorderly persons and thieves.

The citadel of Mont Valerien played a prominent part during the siege of 1871. It not only caused great destruction to the foreign invader, but probably saved the government of M. Thiers from destruction by the Commune, by opening fire upon the insurgents as they marched to Versailles with the intention of capturing the government.

The Palace of St. Cloud (now in ruins) was built in 1658 by Louis XIV., and presented to the Duke of Orleans. It was afterward purchased for Marie Antoinette. Napoleon I. always had a strong liking for the place. In 1825 Blücher had his headquarters at St. Cloud, and the capitulation of Paris was signed there. It was the favorite summer residence of Napoleon III. It was destroyed by fire in 1870.

The French think the Palace of Versailles the finest in the world. It was built, for the most part, by Louis XIV., at a cost of $200,000,000. The front is one-third of a mile in length. When it was finished, half the crowned heads of Europe wanted new palaces. In 1871 Versailles was occupied by the German forces, and on the 18th of January King William, of Prussia, was here proclaimed Emperor of Germany. On the departure of the Germans this palace became the seat of government, under the presidency of M. Thiers, and remained so until the year 1880, when the legislative body returned to Palais Bourbon.

On our return to the city, we called at Sevres. Its principal attraction is the celebrated porcelain factory. Here we had no lecture from the courier. He does not know so much about manufacturers as he does about French history.

Now if any mistakes should be discovered in the foregoing paragraphs, the reader will remember that I am quoting from a garrulous conductor, who was himself repeating somebody's guide book.

The next day we took the tram-car and went out to St. Denis. It was befitting that seven Americans, before taking a final leave of France, should go out to St. Denis, where the kings have been buried from Dagobert I. down to the nineteenth century. And it is not amiss for us to join in the prayer, *Vive la Republique!*

We are glad to know that the kings have been decently laid away in the Cathedral of St. Denis. Here are all the demi-gods— Clovis, Charles Martel, Saint Louis, Henry IV., Francis I., Louis XIV., and the others. On the site where the Cathedral now stands was anciently a chapel in honor of the first Bishop of Paris. It was built A.D. 275.

We shall make some excursions to the various botanical and zoological gardens, and to the numerous libraries and factories hereabout, but there will be no time to write.

We are well prepared for our departure from Europe. Not a mile has been left out of our original itinerary, but many have been added. May we all be as well satisfied to leave the "shores of time!"

From here to Havre; thence to New York; thence home. After the first of September I am at the service of my brethren. I feel like I have a fortune in their friendship. God bless you all.

Paris, August 1, 1891.

RESUME.

Through Europe—Return of Rev. R. A. Young, D.D., and Party—The Great Sights That Were Enjoyed on the Grand Tour—A Close Observer's Comments on Countries and People—Moorish Ruins of Spain, and Oriental Magnificence of Russia.

REV. R. A. YOUNG, D.D., and party returned from their foreign travels Wednesday night. He and his family have made two extended European tours during the last few years, and have visited every country on the continent. The party who made the last trip comprised himself, Mrs. Young, Miss Susie Hunter, Mr. Alex. G. Hunter, Miss Estelle Hart, Miss Marga Davis, and Miss Lale Lester. They left Nashville in January, 1890.

"I suppose you do not want to learn any thing about our voyage across the Atlantic," the Doctor said to a *Herald* reporter who solicited an interview with him yesterday.

"I may say, however, that the Trans-atlantique Line is now regarded as one of the best of the great ocean lines. Their steamers are superb, and they are handled by men who evidently are descended from the Normans.

"Paris is still the social center of the great world of fashion. If you inquire, for instance, where Milan, the ex-King of Servia, resides, you will be told in the French capital. The city and its environs are immensely more beautiful in summer than at any other season. The Bois de Boulogne is the finest park in the world, and St. Cloud, Versailles, and Fontainebleau are the largest royal grounds in Europe. President Carnot does not live at any of them except Fontainebleau, and that is for the pleasure of Madame. The new building for the French Academy is one of the finest structures for the purposes of education and learning that I have seen.

"We made the whole circular tour of Spain, starting at the Bay of Biscay and ending at Marseilles in Southern France. We visited Madrid, the capital; the Escorial, where the Spanish kings and queens are buried; Toledo, Cordova, Seville, and Granada, where there are famous specimens of Moorish architecture, and many other places. It is well known that the Moors of Spain were in their day the best educated and most cultivated people in the world. For 700 years they were the teachers of the great scholars of Europe, who went to them for instruction.

"We spent thirty days among the remains of Moorish civilization at Toledo, Cordova, Seville, and Granada—these are the four charmed spots. The interest and splendor of the ruins the Moors have left are not overrated. The ruins of the Alhambra at Granada are indescribably grand. I was in the rooms occupied by Washington Irving, his library, dining-room, and bed-room; and I brought home a piece of wood from the table on which he wrote 'The Alhambra,' and on which he forged the materials of 'Mohammed and His Successors.'

"At Granada I found 'The Alhambra' printed in English, Spanish, French, German, and Italian, on sale at every news stand

and in the hands of every *valet de place*. The effects of the fire on the palace of the Alhambra, which injured it about a year ago, have been very much exaggerated, and the repairs were completed before we landed. At Toledo, which is called the Pompeii of Spain, there was also a fire a year or two ago, which destroyed the Alcazar, used as a military academy. The Spanish people have a great deal of evidence of their ancient civilization and style.

"There is nothing new to say of cities in Italy, except that Rome bids fair to be 'The Eternal.' Since the location of the Court there, it has been improved according to modern ideas, and it already looks like Paris.

"On our way to Austria and Germany we passed through Switzerland, where preparations were being made to celebrate the 600th anniversary of the Republic. One feature of the celebration was the kindling of a fire on every mountain and hill top of any size in the country.

"Traveling in Russia is very delightful. The country is monotonously level, the stretches very long, and the cars of the most easy and luxurious style. I suppose about one-half of all the royal stuff in Russia may be seen in the Kremlin at Moscow: thrones, robes, crowns, scepters, armor, plate, and jewels by the thousands. One can have no idea of the splendor of a semi-oriental, semi-barbaric capital until he sees Moscow, and gets within the Kremlin walls.

"One-fourth of all the gold produced in the world comes from the mines of Siberia, and they belong to the crown. The Tsars, therefore, can build railroads, palaces, and churches to their heart's content. The people are a very quiet, stately race, but appear to a foreigner like they are too much governed. The music everywhere is of the wailing kind and in a minor key. Eighty-five per cent. of the 110,000,000 population are peasants.

"Our passports were demanded whenever we made a stop. They were carried to the Prefect of Police, and never returned until after we had made a start to leave; we could not get them before. They generally came after we had paid our bill, the hotel-keeper handing them to us. They were *viséed* everywhere. The letters that I wrote to the *Nashville Christian Advocate* about Russia were not mailed until I reached Stockholm, to avoid the possibility of their being read by the censor of the press.

"Stockholm is a grand little capital, and its water-ways make it the Venice of the North. Oscar II. is the only king now reigning that has descended from those made by Napoleon Bonaparte. He is the fourth ruler in the Bernadotte family. From Stockholm we went to Upsala, the site of the great Swedish university, and from there crossed the kingdom to Christiania, where the Norwegian Parliament was discussing political questions as freely as any Democratic Legislature on the face of the earth.

"From Christiania we went by the cariole route to Throndhjem, which is in the latitude of Iceland, and where we saw the "Midnight Sun." The distance was between 300 and 400 miles, and the young people pronounced that the liveliest week of the trip. From Throndhjem we crossed the North Sea to Edinburgh. Then we spent a month in London, and a month in Paris. A person could be interested in London as long as he should stay there. The most astonishing thing about it is its immense size."

Being asked about the morality of Europeans as compared with Americans, Dr. Young said: "If I should place the morality and religion of any part of Europe in comparison with the moral and religious condition of the United States, I would be compelled to give the preference to our own people."

www.ingramcontent.com/pod-product-compliance
Lightning Source LLC
Chambersburg PA
CBHW020259170426
43202CB00008B/443